RETIREMENT ISSUES, PLANS AND LIFESTYLES

401(K) PLANS

ROLLOVER CHALLENGES AND FEE CONSIDERATIONS

RETIREMENT ISSUES, PLANS AND LIFESTYLES

Additional books in this series can be found on Nova's website under the Series tab.

Additional e-books in this series can be found on Nova's website under the e-book tab.

RETIREMENT ISSUES, PLANS AND LIFESTYLES

401(K) PLANS

ROLLOVER CHALLENGES AND FEE CONSIDERATIONS

RUDOLPH GRAHAM
EDITOR

New York

Library of Congress Cataloging-in-Publication Data

ISBN: 978-1-63482-669-3

Published by Nova Science Publishers, Inc. † New York

CONTENTS

PREFACE

This book identifies challenges separating plan participants may face in implementing rollovers; obtaining clear information about which option to choose; and understanding distribution options.

Chapter 1 - 401(k) plan participants separating from their employers must decide what to do with their plan savings. Many roll over their plan savings to IRAs. As GAO previously reported, there is concern that participants may be encouraged to choose rollovers to IRAs in lieu of options that could be more in their interests. Because little attention has been paid to the distribution process, GAO was asked to identify challenges separating plan participants may face in (1) implementing rollovers; (2) obtaining clear information about which option to choose; and (3) understanding distribution options. To answer these questions, GAO reviewed relevant federal laws and regulations, interviewed federal officials and industry experts, conducted a nongeneralizable survey of plan sponsors, and made undercover calls to 401(k) plan service providers to determine what information is provided to plan participants.

Chapter 2 - More and more employees are investing in their futures through 401(k) plans. Employees who participate in 401(k) plans assume responsibility for their retirement income by contributing part of their salary and, in many instances, by directing their own investments.

If you are among those who direct your investments, you will need to consider the investment objectives, the risk and return characteristics, and the performance over time of each investment option offered by your plan in order to make sound investment decisions. Fees and expenses are one of the factors that will affect your investment returns and will impact your retirement income.

The information contained in this chapter answers some common questions about the fees and expenses that may be paid by your 401(k) plan. It highlights the most common fees and encourages you, as a 401(k) plan participant, to:

- Make informed investment decisions;
- Consider fees as one of several factors in your decision making;
- Compare all services received with the total cost; and
- Realize that cheaper is not necessarily better.

Keep in mind, however, that this chapter is a simplified explanation of some common 401(k) fees. It is not a legal interpretation of the nation's major retirement benefits protection law, the Employee Retirement Income Security Act (ERISA), or other laws, nor is this information intended to be investment advice.

In: 401(k) Plans
Editor: Rudolph Graham

ISBN: 978-1-63482-669-3

Chapter 1

401(K) PLANS: LABOR AND IRS COULD IMPROVE THE ROLLOVER PROCESS FOR PARTICIPANTS*

United States Government Accountability Office

WHY GAO DID THIS STUDY

401(k) plan participants separating from their employers must decide what to do with their plan savings. Many roll over their plan savings to IRAs. As GAO previously reported, there is concern that participants may be encouraged to choose rollovers to IRAs in lieu of options that could be more in their interests. Because little attention has been paid to the distribution process, GAO was asked to identify challenges separating plan participants may face in (1) implementing rollovers; (2) obtaining clear information about which option to choose; and (3) understanding distribution options. To answer these questions, GAO reviewed relevant federal laws and regulations, interviewed federal officials and industry experts, conducted a nongeneralizable survey of plan sponsors, and made undercover calls to 401(k) plan service providers to determine what information is provided to plan participants.

---

* This is an edited, reformatted and augmented version of a United States Government Accountability Office publication, No. GAO-13-30, dated March 2013.

WHAT GAO RECOMMENDS

Among other things, GAO recommends that Labor and IRS should take certain steps to reduce obstacles and disincentives to planto-plan rollovers. Labor should also ensure that participants receive complete and timely information, including enhanced disclosures, about the distribution options for their 401(k) plan savings when separating from an employer. In response, Labor and Treasury generally agreed with the findings and will explore ways to implement these recommendations.

WHAT GAO FOUND

The current rollover process favors distributions to individual retirement accounts (IRA). Waiting periods to roll into a new employer plan, complex verification procedures to ensure savings are tax-qualified, wide divergences in plans' paperwork, and inefficient practices for processing rollovers make IRA rollovers an easier and faster choice, especially given that IRA providers often offer assistance to plan participants when they roll their savings into an IRA. The Department of Labor (Labor) and the Internal Revenue Service (IRS) provide oversight and guidance for this process generally and can take steps to make plan-to-plan rollovers more efficient, such as reducing the waiting period to roll over into a 401(k) plan and improving the asset verification process. Such actions could help make staying in the 401(k) plan environment a more viable option, allowing participants to make distribution decisions based on their financial circumstances rather than on convenience.

Plan participants often receive guidance and marketing favoring IRAs when seeking assistance regarding what to do with their 401(k) plan savings when they separate from their employers. GAO found that service providers' call center representatives encouraged rolling 401(k) plan savings into an IRA even with only minimal knowledge of a caller's financial situation. Participants may also interpret information about their plans' service providers' retail investment products contained in their plans' educational materials as suggestions to choose those products. Labor's current requirements do not sufficiently assist participants in understanding the financial interests that service providers may have in participants' distribution and investment decisions.

In addition to being subject to inefficient rollover processes and the marketing of IRAs, 401(k) plan participants separating from their employers may find it difficult to understand and compare all their distribution options. Information participants currently receive is either too generic and without detail, leaving participants without understanding of the key factors they need to know to make decisions about their savings, or too long and technical, leaving participants overwhelmed and confused. Labor regulations do not ensure that 401(k) plans provide complete and timely information to participants on all their distribution options. Industry experts told GAO that participants could benefit from simplified, concise, and standardized information.

ABBREVIATIONS

EBSA	Employee Benefits Security Administration
ERISA	Employee Retirement Income Security Act of 1974
FINRA	Financial Industry Regulatory Authority
ICI	Investment Company Institute
IRA	individual retirement account
IRC	Internal Revenue Code
IRS	Internal Revenue Service
Labor	Department of Labor
SEC	Securities and Exchange Commission
Treasury	Department of the Treasury

* * *

March 7, 2013

The Honorable Tom Harkin
Chairman
Committee on Health, Education, Labor and Pensions
United States Senate

The Honorable Bill Nelson
Chairman
Special Committee on Aging
United States Senate

The Honorable George Miller
Ranking Member
Committee on Education and the Workforce
United States House of Representatives

When participants in employer-sponsored 401(k) plans separate from an employer, rolling their funds into an individual retirement account (IRA) is one of several options available to them. Rollovers to IRAs from 401(k) plans are a common investment choice for plan participants and they are frequently advertised on television and in multiple venues.[1] Rollovers from 401(k) plans and other employer-sponsored retirement plans are so prevalent that they are the predominant source of contributions to IRAs. Approximately 95 percent of money contributed to traditional IRAs in 2008 was from rollovers, primarily from employer-sponsored retirement plans.[2] Yet, the choice to roll over 401(k) plan savings into an IRA may or may not be in the best interest of participants depending on their individual circumstances. Despite the growth in IRA rollovers, very little is known about how the distribution process of 401(k) plan savings came to be centered on rolling savings into an IRA. Our past work has highlighted concern that 401(k) plan participants may be encouraged to roll over plan balances to IRAs without understanding or considering other options. Consequently, you asked that we identify some of the challenges plan participants separating from their employers may face.

This report examines the challenges plan participants face in (1) implementing a rollover, including plan-to-plan rollovers;[3] (2) getting accurate and clear information about which distribution option to choose for their 401(k) plan retirement savings; and (3) understanding their distribution options.

To answer these objectives we used a variety of data collection methods. To understand the rollover marketplace, we reviewed relevant research and data from a variety of academic and industry-based sources. To understand the extent of laws and regulations on the rollover process, we reviewed federal laws and regulations pertaining to 401(k) plans and IRAs; met with government officials from the Department of Labor (Labor), the Department of the Treasury (Treasury), the Internal Revenue Service (IRS), and the Consumer Financial Protection Bureau; and met with 401(k) plan service providers (many of which offer retail IRAs), 401(k) plan sponsors, and other experts. To understand the role of 401(k) plan service providers in participants' decision-making processes, we conducted 29 structured interviews with 401(k) plan service providers, including those with the largest assets under management. In addition, working with three industry-based membership organizations, we collected written responses to questions used in our interviews from 25 additional service provider firms. (See appendix I for more information.) To understand the role and perspectives of 401(k) plan sponsors with regard to the rollover process, we conducted a non-generalizable survey, facilitated through two member organizations: PLANSPONSOR and the Society for Human Resource Management. We received a total of 76 responses to our survey and we also interviewed five plan sponsors. To assess the content and availability of information available to individuals, we reviewed 10 IRA providers' websites for account fees and rollover promotions. We also investigated the guidance and information that plan service providers give to individuals through calls placed by our investigative unit to 30 401(k) plan service providers representing those with the largest 401(k) assets under management. 27 of the 30 service providers also offer IRAs, including those with the largest IRA assets under management. During the calls our investigator asked about rollover options and processes, and IRA costs. In addition, we used research and data from a variety of pension and investment industry-based sources to answer our research questions. Though much of the data we obtained are not generalizable, together they provide a rich source of relevant information. For more information on the data and other methodologies we used see appendix I.

We conducted this performance audit from May 2011 to March 2013 in accordance with generally accepted government auditing standards. Those standards require that we plan and perform the audit to obtain sufficient, appropriate evidence to provide a reasonable basis for our findings and conclusions based on our audit objectives. We believe that the evidence obtained provides a reasonable basis for findings and conclusions based on our audit objectives. We conducted our related investigative work in accordance with standards prescribed by the Council of Inspectors General on Integrity and Efficiency.

BACKGROUND

401(k) Plans

Congress has established tax incentives to encourage employers to sponsor retirement plans and employees to participate in them.[4] Under the Employee Retirement Income Security Act of 1974 (ERISA),[5] employers may sponsor two broad types of retirement plans, referred to in ERISA as pension plans:[6] (1) defined benefit plans,[7] which promise to provide benefits generally based on an employee's years of service and frequently are based on salary, regardless of the performance of the plans' investments, and (2) defined contribution plans, in which benefits are based on contributions and the performance of the investments in participants' individual accounts.[8]

Over the last three decades, employers have shifted away from sponsoring defined benefit plans and toward defined contribution plans. The 401(k) plan is the predominant type of defined contribution plan in the United States. In 2010, employers sponsored over 510,000 401(k) plans with participation from over 60 million workers.[9] The assets held in these plans totaled more than $3.1 trillion.[10]

Typically, 401(k) plans allow participants to specify the size of their contributions and direct those contributions, as well as any made by their employer, to one or more investments among the options offered within the plan. Investment choices within the plan generally include options such as mutual funds, target date funds (which are designed to reduce the risk of investment losses as a participant approaches their "target" retirement date), stable value funds (which are designed to preserve the participants' contributions, or their principal, while also providing steady positive returns), company stock, and money market funds. Industry research shows that, as of the end of 2009, participants had allocated about 41 percent of 401(k) plan assets to equity funds, a type of mutual fund that mainly invests in stocks, followed by a mix of other investments, including company stock and stable value funds.[11] When deciding how to allocate assets among the various investment options, experts generally advise that participants consider a number of factors, such as historical performance, investment risk, fees associated with each option, and various individual circumstances, such as the time horizon to retirement. As we have previously reported, even a seemingly small fee, such as a 1 percent annual charge, can significantly reduce 401(k) plan savings over the course of a participant's career.[12]

Plan sponsors often hire companies to provide the services necessary to operate their 401(k) plans.[13] Some of these services—such as investment management, consulting and providing financial advice, recordkeeping, and custodial or trustee services for plan assets—are provided directly to plan sponsors. Services are also provided to participants, such as offering financial advice, assisting with processing transactions, or providing educational information.

Advisory services for participants can be provided through a variety of methods, including call centers or help desks, group seminars, one-on-one sessions, computer models, or brochures and other printed materials.

Individual Retirement Accounts

Individual retirement accounts—popularly known as IRAs—have grown in importance and have become key retirement savings vehicles for many individuals, including small business owners, independent contractors, and other workers not covered by an employer-sponsored pension plan.

IRA assets totaled $5.1 trillion by mid-year 2012, accounting for 28 percent of U.S. retirement assets, according to the Investment Company Institute (ICI). 14 Created by ERISA, traditional IRAs were established to (1) provide a way for individuals not covered by a pension plan to save for retirement, and (2) give retiring workers or individuals changing jobs a way to preserve assets from employer-sponsored retirement plans by allowing them to roll over, or transfer, plan balances into IRAs.

Additionally, the Taxpayer Relief Act of 1997 created Roth IRAs.[15] These two types of IRAs are described in table 1.

Table 1. Two Types of IRAs

Traditional IRAs 26 U.S.C. § 408 (a), (d) and (o).	Eligible individuals may make tax-deductible contributions but distributions after age 59%, when individuals are more likely to be retired and in a lower tax bracket, are generally subject to income tax. Distributions made before age 59%, other than under specific exceptions,[a] are also subject to income tax, but in addition, are generally subject to a tax equal to 10 percent of the distribution. Any individual may make non-deductible contributions and, in such cases, after age 59%, only the portion of distributions derived from investment earnings is subject to income tax. Yearly contribution amounts are subject to limits based, for example, on income and pension coverage. Retirees over age 70% cannot make additional contributions and must begin receiving required minimum distributions.

Table 1. (Continued)

Roth IRAs 26 U.S.C. § 408A.	Eligible individuals may make contributions that are not tax-deductible but after 5 years distributions made after age 59% are not subject to income tax (beyond what was already paid on contributions). The portion of distributions made before age 59% derived from investment earnings are generally subject to income tax and, generally, an additional tax equal to 10 percent of that portion. Yearly contributions are subject to limits based, for example, on income, filing status and any contributions to a traditional IRA. There are, however, no age limits on contributing and no distributions are required during the individual's lifetime.

Source: GAO analysis.

[a] These exceptions include, for example, withdrawals for certain higher education expenses and first home purchase. 26 U.S.C. § 72(t)(2)(E) and (F).

Rollover Process

When 401(k) plan participants separate from their employers, they generally have up to four options for their plan savings: leave the money in the plan, roll or move the money into a new qualified employer plan, roll the money into an IRA, or take a lump sum distribution ("cash out"[16]).[17] (See figure 1.)

The first three options allow a participant to preserve the tax-deferred status of their plan savings. In contrast, the Internal Revenue Code (IRC) imposes an additional tax of 10 percent (in addition to ordinary income tax) on cash outs made from qualified retirement plans, which includes 401(k) plans and IRAs, before a participant reaches age 591/2,[18] in order to discourage the use of plan funds for purposes other than retirement and ensure that the favorable tax treatment for plan funds is limited to those that are, in fact, used to provide retirement income.[19] In addition, employers must withhold 20 percent of the cash outs to cover anticipated income tax.[20]

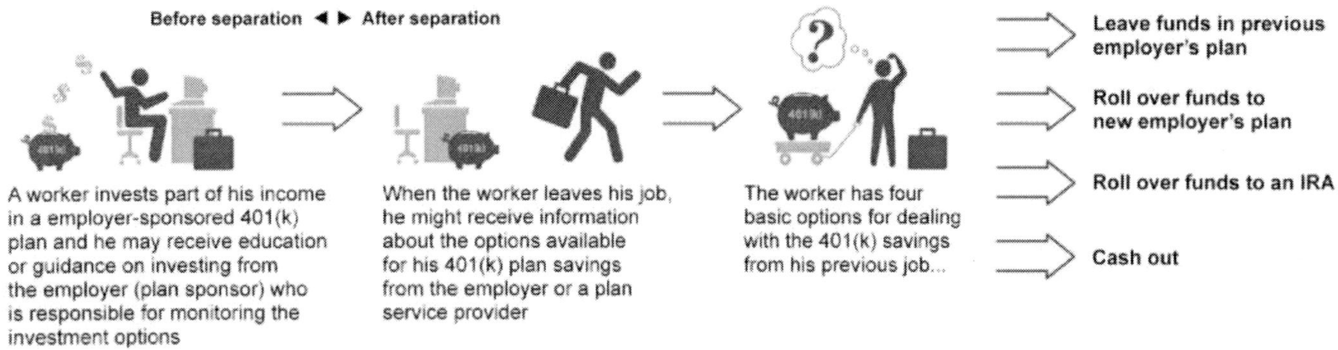

Source: GAO analysis.

Note: Plans are not always required to permit separated participants to leave funds in the plan once they separate from employment if the balance is less than $5,000 or if the participant attains the later of age 62 or the normal retirement age. Plans are also not required to accept rollovers. Participants must check with the new plan's administrator to determine if the plan permits rollovers into the plan. In some cases, participants may be offered the option to annuitize their 401(k) plan savings at annuity purchase rates offered through the plan if they are retiring. However, after such a purchase, participants typically are no longer plan participants and their annuity benefit is the responsibility of the insurance company from which the annuity is purchased.

Figure 1. Separating 401(k) Plan Participants Generally Have Up to Four Options for Their Plan Savings.

A 401(k) plan can complete a direct rollover[21] in either of two ways: (1) by sending the funds directly to the new employer's retirement plan or to an IRA, or (2) by mailing the departing participant a check that must be made payable to the new plan or IRA, and that the participant then has to deliver to the new plan or IRA. An indirect rollover involves the current (soon to be former) 401(k) plan issuing the departing participant a check, payable to the participant, who then has 60 days from the date of receipt to either cash the check and write a new check to the new employer's retirement plan or an IRA, or endorse the distribution check and mail it to the new employer's retirement plan or an IRA.[22] A plan could also send the distributed funds electronically to a participant's bank account and the new retirement plan or IRA might allow the participant to electronically transfer the funds into their new account. As a cash distribution, the 20 percent withholding for anticipated taxes applies, but the regular income tax and additional 10 percent tax do not apply to the funds rolled into a new employer plan or IRA. The implications of these alternative procedures are discussed later in this report.

While many participants take distributions from plans when they separate from employment, others may wait to take such distributions at a later date. For instance, industry data on participants in defined contribution plans aged 60 years and over who separated from employment in 2004 show that about 50 percent of their plan savings remained in employer plans 1 year after separating, but only about 20 percent of their plan savings remained in the plans 5 years after separating.[23]

Rollovers have become the largest source of contributions to IRAs. According to ICI, from 1996 to 2008, over 90 percent of funds flowing into traditional IRAs came from rollovers primarily from employer-sponsored retirement plans.[24] ICI reported that, in 2012, 51 percent of the traditional IRAs held by 20 million U.S. households included rollover funds.[25] In 2012, for 47 percent of households with traditional IRA accounts that included rollover funds, rollover funds from employer-sponsored retirement plans accounted for 75 percent or more of the account balance. Furthermore, the market for rollover dollars is large and competitive. Numerous reports and news articles that we reviewed address "rollover opportunities" and include strategies for retaining and capturing assets rolling out of plans.

Oversight of 401(k) Plans

401(k) plans are subject to various provisions of ERISA, which are generally enforced by Labor's Employee Benefits Security Administration (EBSA) and Treasury's Internal Revenue Service (IRS). ERISA was enacted to, among other things, protect the interests of plan participants and their beneficiaries and set minimum standards for most private sector pension plans. 26 To carry out its responsibilities, EBSA issues regulations and other guidance, conducts investigations of plan fiduciaries and service providers, and seeks appropriate remedies to correct violations of the law. To assist regulated parties in complying with ERISA, EBSA also educates plan participants, beneficiaries, and plan sponsors. ERISA established standards of conduct for plan fiduciaries, which include plan sponsors.[27] Fiduciaries generally must act solely in the interest of plan participants and beneficiaries for the exclusive purpose of providing plan benefits and defraying the expense of plan administration.[28]

Depending on the functions that service providers perform for a plan, they may also be plan fiduciaries and are then subject to the same standards outlined in ERISA and its regulations. When providing assistance to participants, a service provider may furnish investment advice or investment education. Investment advice, under a current Labor regulation, consists of investment recommendations provided on a regular basis, and with both parties understanding that the recommendations are individualized and will serve as the primary basis for investment decisions.[29] Investment education consists of general investment information, including general information about the plan and asset allocation models that is not tailored to the needs or interests of an individual plan participant. In a 2005 advisory opinion under this regulation, however, Labor took the view that advice to take an otherwise permissible distribution, even if combined with a recommendation on how to invest it, would not trigger fiduciary status, unless the person providing such recommendations were already an ERISA fiduciary.[30] Furthermore, Labor's interpretive bulletin relating to participant investment education indicates that service providers may use their own retail investment products as examples in informational materials for plan participants without such information constituting investment advice, as long as certain required statements are made in the materials.[31]

On October 22, 2010, Labor proposed a revision to its definition of an ERISA "fiduciary" to account for changes in the financial industry and the expectations of plan officials and participants who receive investment advice.[32] The proposed regulation would have reduced the number of conditions that need to be met to be deemed an ERISA fiduciary and permitted oversight with respect to a broader range of service providers. The preamble to the proposed revised definition notes that, as a general matter, a recommendation to a plan participant to take an otherwise permissible distribution does not constitute investment advice within the meaning of the current regulation even when that advice is combined with a recommendation as to how the distribution should be invested. It also notes, however, concerns that plan participants may not be adequately protected from advisers who provide distribution recommendations that subordinate participants' interests to the advisers' own interests. Comments on the proposed rule, specifically including on whether and to what extent the final regulation should define the provision of investment advice to encompass recommendations related to taking a plan distribution, were originally due at Labor on or before January 20, 2011, but that deadline was extended two weeks to February 3, 2011.[33]

In March 2011, EBSA held a hearing to consider issues attendant to adopting its proposed rule on when a person is considered to be an ERISA fiduciary by reason of giving investment advice to an employee benefit plan or to a plan's participants and beneficiaries. In September 2011, citing requests from the public, including members of Congress, that Labor allow an opportunity for more input on the rule, Labor announced that it would withdraw its October 22, 2010 proposed rule. Labor indicated, at that time, that it would repropose its rule on the definition of a fiduciary in early 2012, but as yet has not done so. Labor currently anticipates that its reproposal will be issued in 2013. In addition, the IRC sets out standards that 401(k) plans must meet to receive preferential tax treatment, and these are enforced by the IRS, as described in greater detail below.

Enforcement of IRA Requirements

The IRS has primary responsibility for ensuring that 401(k) plans and IRAs meet IRC requirements, related to, for example, their establishment and operation, as necessary to qualify for the preferential tax treatments available to them.[34] The IRS is also responsible for imposing a tax on disqualified persons (which includes, for example, plan sponsors or service providers) who engage in certain prohibited transactions indicative of self-dealing or conflicts of interest with plans, while in the case of an IRA, this tax is not imposed but the IRA's favorable tax treatment is eliminated.[35] Such prohibited transactions specifically include, for example, borrowing money from an IRA, selling property to an IRA, receiving unreasonable compensation from an IRA for managing the account, using an IRA account as security for a loan, and buying property for personal use with IRA funds. Based on ERISA provisions generally prohibiting pension plans from engaging in largely the same transactions that subject disqualified persons to taxation, [36] Labor shares responsibility for enforcing prohibited transaction requirements with IRS and, under Reorganization Plan No.4 of 1978, has the authority to apply the statutory exemptions and grant additional exemptions under certain circumstances.[37] If an individual for whom an IRA was established engages in a prohibited transaction, such as using the IRA as security for a loan or buying property for personal use with IRA funds, the IRA loses its status as an IRA and is therefore disqualified from favorable tax treatment.[38]

Labor's Recent Fee Disclosure Requirements

Other recent regulatory initiatives focus on enhanced disclosure to plan fiduciaries and plan participants. These regulations, as described in table 2, enhance the disclosure of plan financial information related to fees and other arrangements involving plan fiduciaries and participants.

Table 2. Summary of Final Rules for Labor's Disclosure Initiatives

Reasonable Contract or Arrangement Under Section 408(b)(2)–Fee Disclosure, 77 Fed. Reg. 5632, 5655-58 (Feb. 3, 2012) (codified at 29 C.F.R. § 2550.408b-2(c) (2012))	ERISA prohibits contracts between a plan and a party in interest unless they are reasonable, services provided under them are necessary to the plan, and no more than reasonable compensation is paid for those services. 29 U.S.C. §§ 1106(a)(1)(C) and 1108(b)(2). Regulations effective July 1, 2012 prescribe disclosures about service fees, among other things, that must be furnished to plan fiduciaries, such as plan sponsors, in order for contracts to be considered reasonable.
Fiduciary Requirements for Disclosure in Participant-Directed Individual Account Plans, 75 Fed. Reg. 64,910, 64,937-46 (Oct. 20, 2010) (codified as amended at 29 C.F.R. §§ 2550.404a5 and 2550.404c-1 (2012))	Where plan participants and beneficiaries are responsible for allocation and investment of their plan assets, as in 401(k) plans, plan sponsors and other fiduciaries must take steps to ensure that participants and beneficiaries are regularly made aware of those responsibilities and provided sufficient plan information, including information about fees and expenses, to make informed decisions regarding management of their accounts. Regulations effective Dec. 20, 2010, prescribe specific fiduciary requirements for disclosures that plan administrators must provide in order for participants and beneficiaries to have sufficient plan information.

Source: GAO analysis of Labor regulations.

Other Rules Affecting 401(k) Plan and IRA Investments

The specific investment products held in 401(k) plans and IRAs, as well as the various financial professionals that service them, are subject to oversight from applicable securities, banking, or insurance regulators, which can include both federal and state regulators. For example, mutual funds, offered in both plans and IRAs, are generally regulated by the Securities and Exchange Commission (SEC), which requires funds to disclose fees and to inform investors of products' potential risks. An investment adviser provides a wide range of investment advisory services, including management of client portfolios. Investment advisers manage the portfolios of individuals as well as the portfolios of pension funds and mutual funds. Broker-dealers provide brokerage services where they act as an agent for someone else; a dealer acts as a principal for its own account. SEC has primary responsibility for oversight of investment advisers and broker-dealers, while those who sell insurance products are also subject to state insurance regulation.[39] Investment advisers, broker-dealers, and insurance agents are subject to different standards of practice, and for anyone servicing a 401(k) plan ERISA standards may also apply.

According to SEC, all investment advisers—whether registered with SEC or not—have a fiduciary obligation under the Investment Advisers Act of 1940, which includes duties of loyalty and care and to serve the best interests of its clients. [40] As part of its fiduciary duty, the investment adviser is required to avoid conflicts of interest and, at a minimum, make full disclosure of material conflicts of interest to their clients. When an adviser fails to disclose information regarding material conflicts of interest, clients are unable to make informed decisions about entering into or continuing the advisory relationship. SEC also regulates broker-dealers under the Securities Exchange Act of 1934, which generally requires that broker-dealers register with SEC, unless an exception or exemption applies.[41] In addition, broker-dealers that deal with the public generally must become members of the Financial Industry Regulatory Authority, Inc. (FINRA). Under the anti-fraud provisions of the federal securities laws, broker-dealers are required to deal fairly with their customers and meet a suitability standard when rendering investment recommendations.[42] Consequently, when a broker-dealer makes a recommendation to buy, exchange, or sell a security to a retail investor, that broker-dealer must recommend only those securities that the broker reasonably believes are suitable for the customer. In addition, a broker-dealer must disclose all material information regarding the security and the recommendation, including, among other things, any material conflicts of interest. Additionally, broker-dealers are restricted from participating in certain transactions that present particularly acute potential conflicts of interest.

The Dodd-Frank Wall Street Reform and Consumer Protection Act requires the SEC to conduct a study on the effectiveness of the existing standards of care for broker-dealers and investment advisers. 43 Based on its review, SEC staff recommended that SEC propose rules that apply a uniform standard of conduct which requires broker-dealers and investment advisers, when providing personalized investment advice to retail customers, to act in the best interest of the customer without regard to the financial or other interest of the broker, dealer, or investment adviser. SEC staff also recommended that SEC should facilitate the provision of uniform, simple, and clear disclosures to retail customers about the terms of their relationships with broker-dealers and investment advisers.[44] (For more information on securities laws, see GAO-11-119.)[45]

If SEC decides to impose a uniform fiduciary standard on investment advisers and broker-dealers when providing personalized investment advice to retail customers, this standard could differ from the fiduciary standard applicable to ERISA fiduciaries. While investment advisers must act in the best interests of their clients, ERISA fiduciaries are required to act in the sole interest of plan participants and beneficiaries for the exclusive purpose of providing benefits and defraying administrative costs. Additionally, although ERISA prohibits certain transactions, such as sales of securities to plans by fiduciaries, the Advisers Act permits investment advisers to engage in these sales as long as disclosures are made and consent is obtained.

Direct Rollover Process Can Be Inefficient and Encourages Participants to Choose the IRA Option

401(k) plan processes for handling separating participants' accounts create barriers for participants to roll their savings to a new plan, making IRA rollovers an easier and faster choice for those who want to consolidate their savings in a new account after they separate from an employer. Currently, plans may include waiting periods before processing a new employee's rollover and have long and complex processes for verifying the tax-qualified status of the savings to be rolled over. Barriers to rolling 401(k) plan savings to a new plan include:

- **Rollover waiting period**. When joining a 401(k) plan with a new employer, several service providers told us that participants may find the new plan requires a waiting period prior to rolling in old 401(k) plan balances. These waiting periods are at the discretion of the plan and can last weeks or months. Treasury and IRS officials said that while plans see the delays as an administrative necessity, the delays create uncertainty for participants and complicate the rollover process. In contrast, several service provider representatives pointed out to our investigator that their companies' IRAs require no such waiting period when rolling over funds. Consistent with the IRC and ERISA, IRS and Labor have largely left plan sponsors free to follow their own practices about when and how they will allow rollovers into their plans.
- **Complex verification process**. Plans can require complex and lengthy verification processes for rollover funds to ensure they are tax-qualified. For example, they can request a participant's previous plan complete verification forms, but that plan has little incentive to handle the verification in a timely way. Participants may be responsible for ensuring that their former employers' plans complete and return the verification forms. The IRS publishes requirements that plans must meet to maintain their qualified status. This status benefits both participants and the plan sponsors. One requirement is that plans hold only tax-qualified money. Treasury and IRS officials told us that plan sponsors discouraging rollovers from old plans is a problem, which may result from their concerns that accepting rollover funds from other plans will result in inadvertently taking in non-qualified money into their 401(k) plans, which could violate IRS rules and result in loss of a plan's qualified status. But Treasury and IRS officials said that plan sponsors who are acting reasonably should not be fearful about accepting non-qualified money into their plans, because if such errors are identified, typically they can be corrected without penalty. IRS regulations provide that as long as a plan that receives rollover funds "reasonably concludes" that they came from a qualified plan, and as long as the funds are removed from the plan, the receiving plan's qualified status would not be at risk even if it is later concluded that the funds came from a plan that was not qualified.[46]

One plan sponsor told us that only 10 to 15 percent of participants who separate from the plan move their savings to a new employer's plan because of barriers in the process, including many paper forms and the involvement of both plan administrators. Furthermore, experts we interviewed said that these barriers in the process make plan-to-plan rollovers more difficult for participants. That difficulty may discourage participants from keeping their savings in the plan environment, which generally has lower fees, better comparative information, and ERISA plan fiduciaries required to select and monitor reasonable investment options.

A lack of a standardized process also adds to the complexity of the rollover process, which burdens participants and gives an advantage to IRA providers who have the resources and financial incentive to provide more rollover assistance than plan sponsors. Even participants with past rollover experience may have no idea what information their current plans' distribution forms will require, how long the previous employers' plans will take to process a distribution request, or how the receiving plans will process a direct rollover request. More than half of service providers we interviewed who had suggestions for improving the rollover process (19 of 35 with suggestions) said regulators could improve the rollover process by simplifying it. One plan adviser told us that half of participants need help filling out the distribution paperwork.

- **Paperwork differences**. Several service providers told us that plans use different distribution forms, which may confuse participants. Labor does not require 401(k) plans to use standardized distribution paperwork. Some service providers suggested that using standardized distribution forms or electronic forms to process the rollover request would be one way to simplify the process. We reviewed 14 packets of sample distribution materials provided to plan participants and found that the size and content of the packets varied. Several were single documents of only a few pages, while others included multiple documents, with three exceeding 15 pages in total. More than half of the packets did not include a distribution request form, burdening the participants by forcing them to contact their plans or service providers to request the necessary forms.
- **Processing time differences**. The length of time it takes to complete a distribution of a participant's 401(k) plan balance largely depends on the service provider for the plan. Neither IRS nor Labor requires 401(k) plans to process distribution requests in a specified time frame. Several service providers told us that because it is not in the interests of most service providers to release funds to another service provider

> they may not process such requests expeditiously. One service provider filed a complaint with FINRA to pressure another service provider to release 401(k) plan funds for a rollover. An individual participant is unlikely to know how to apply the same pressure when faced with inexplicable delays. Unless required to process a distribution within a specified time frame, plans and their service providers will continue to make this task a low priority, leaving participants uncertain about the status of their retirement savings.

In addition, industry experts said that the direct-rollover process is often inefficient, taking more time and effort than is necessary, whether the participant is rolling over to another plan or rolling into an IRA. As shown in figure 2, during a direct rollover, when separating participants request that their current plan transfer their plan savings to a specific new plan or IRA, many plans and service providers route the distribution check (which is made payable only to the receiving entity) through the participant who must then forward it to their new plan or IRA. Experts noted that the inefficiency of processing direct rollovers this way burdens participants choosing to roll over their plan savings. This process can result in their checks getting misplaced or lost, which is more likely if someone is relocating for a new job. Direct rollovers processed this way rely on individuals to play a crucial role in routing their retirement plan savings to a receiving entity, which, if they make a mistake, results in confusion for the individual who thinks their money is invested when it is not or who may not know where their plan savings are located. In addition, this practice prolongs the length of time it takes to process the rollover. A participant's money may be in process for weeks given the time it takes a service provider to prepare and send a check and forward it by mail, first to a participant and then on to a receiving plan or IRA. Such processing delays increase the likelihood that a participant will not complete the rollover process, leaving his or her retirement accounts unconsolidated and harder to manage.

Treasury and IRS officials said that 401(k) plan service providers often choose to send direct-rollover distribution checks to participants rather than to the receiving institutions, because it is easier for the service provider. Although IRS requires plans that receive a direct-rollover request to issue non-transferable checks payable to the receiving plan or IRA, regulations expressly allow the distributing plans to send the check itself to the separating participants, making participants responsible for completing the rollover and shifting the administrative burden from the record-keepers,[47] who are well-suited to manage the task, to individuals who may not know what steps to take.[48]

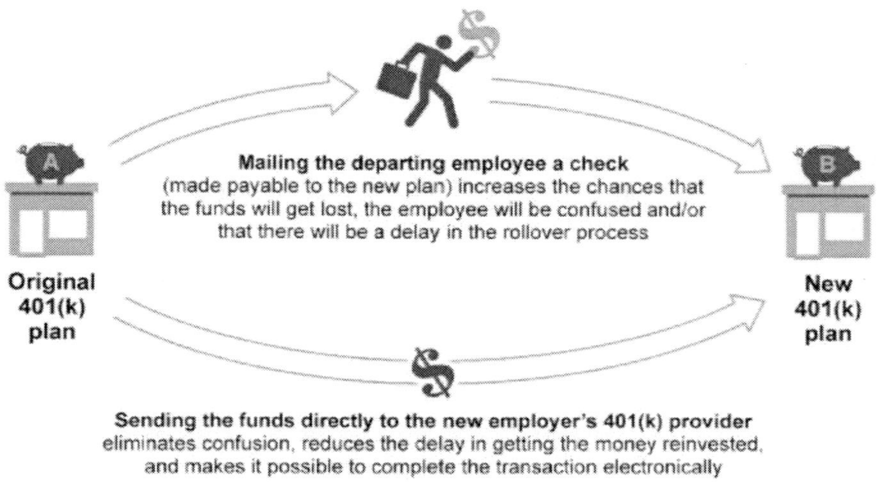

Source: GAO analysis.

Note: The same processes are used for 401(k) plan rollovers to IRAs. Not every institution may accept rollovers electronically.

Figure 2. Two Ways 401(k) Plans May Process Direct Rollovers to a New Plan.

Although rolling directly into an IRA can also require participants to act as intermediaries by receiving and relaying their checks, IRA providers offer participants assistance with the rollover process, making it as easy as possible. A third (10 of 30) of the 401(k) plan service providers called by our investigator seeking information about options for his 401(k) plan savings at his ex-employer's plan offered to assist the caller with an IRA rollover, but just one of those offered to assist with a plan-to-plan rollover. Some firms' representatives provided their direct phone numbers for the caller to use if he had questions or when he was ready to roll over to an IRA and others highlighted the complexity of the rollover process, offering to help with the paperwork. For example, one firm filled out portions of the rollover paperwork for the caller and e-mailed it to him, noting places where he would need to add information or sign. According to one industry survey of participants with savings at a former employer's plan, online research is a key source of information for those researching their rollover options, providing another venue for IRA providers to promote the relative ease of an IRA rollover and the assistance they provide with processing a rollover.[49]

We found that it is common for IRA providers to offer assistance with a rollover to their IRA. Our review of 10 IRA providers' websites found that 9 providers advertise their assistance with processing an IRA rollover. Several providers advertise that someone could roll over to their IRA in 15 minutes or less. For example, one provider contacted by our investigator claimed that an individual can complete the online IRA rollover application in 10 minutes. Cash bonuses for an individual rolling over funds are another incentive to roll over to a particular IRA provider. In our analysis of providers' websites we found bonuses that ranged from $50 to $2,500, depending on the individual's amount of savings. According to a large but non-generalizable survey of individuals eligible to rollover, of those surveyed who had rolled over savings to an IRA, 68 percent rated "quick and easy process to open the account" as important to their decisions and 52 percent gave "assistance in completing the forms to open the account" the same high rating.[50] Another study found that the most popular reason participants gave for selecting an IRA provider was that it made rolling over easy.[51] Additionally, a service provider that assists plan participants in rolling over their savings told us that, when plans or their service providers provide such assistance, a large proportion of participants chose to consolidate their old accounts in the new 401(k) plan.

PARTICIPANTS ARE SUBJECTED TO PERVASIVE MARKETING OF IRAS, BUT MAY RECEIVE LIMITED ASSISTANCE REGARDING THEIR DISTRIBUTION OPTIONS

Many experts told us that much of the information and assistance participants receive is through the marketing efforts of service providers touting the benefits of IRA rollovers and is not always objective. Plan participants are often subject to biased information and aggressive marketing of IRAs when seeking assistance and information regarding what to do with their 401(k) plan savings when they separate or have separated from employment with a plan sponsor. In many cases, such information and marketing come from plan service providers. As we have reported in the past, the opportunity for service providers to sell participants their own retail investment products and services, such as IRAs, may create an incentive for service providers to steer participants toward the purchase of such products and services even when they may not serve the participants' best interests.[52]

With respect to asset allocation of current plan investment options, according to EBSA's 1996 interpretive bulletin on investment advice and investment education, service providers may present specific investment alternatives under 401(k) plans— including those in which the provider has a financial interest—as examples of investments available under an asset class when presenting asset allocation models as part of investment education.[53] The bulletin specifies that a model identifying a specific investment alternative available under the plan would not constitute a "recommendation" if accompanied by statements indicating that (1) the plan may offer investment alternatives with similar risk and return and where to find information on those investments, and (2) participants or beneficiaries, in applying particular asset allocation models to their individual situations, should consider their other assets, income, and investments in addition to their interests in the plan.[54] Accordingly, presenting specific investment options would not constitute provision of "investment advice," and therefore would not trigger ERISA fiduciary status, which would require the service provider to act solely in the best interest of the plan participants.[55] In the bulletin, EBSA contends that such statements would enable a participant or beneficiary to assess the relevance of an asset allocation model to his or her individual situation.

Even with disclosure statements as required in the bulletin, participants may interpret information about their plans providers' retail investment products contained in their plans' educational materials as suggestions or recommendations to choose those products.[56] Research has shown that many individuals contributing to defined contribution plans or IRAs spend very little time scrutinizing disclosure statements.[57] Furthermore, as we have previously reported, consumers may not understand the differences among various types of financial services professionals (including the different standards of care they must adhere to), or that those professionals may have conflicts of interest when providing guidance or selling products.[58] Because of a lack of understanding of the distinction between investment education and investment advice or of the standards plan providers must adhere to when giving information or assistance, participants may believe that providers are giving them investment advice and that it is being provided in their best interest. As shown in figure 3, a provider's offer of their own retail IRA in a plan's distribution materials is one way to guide participants into their products.

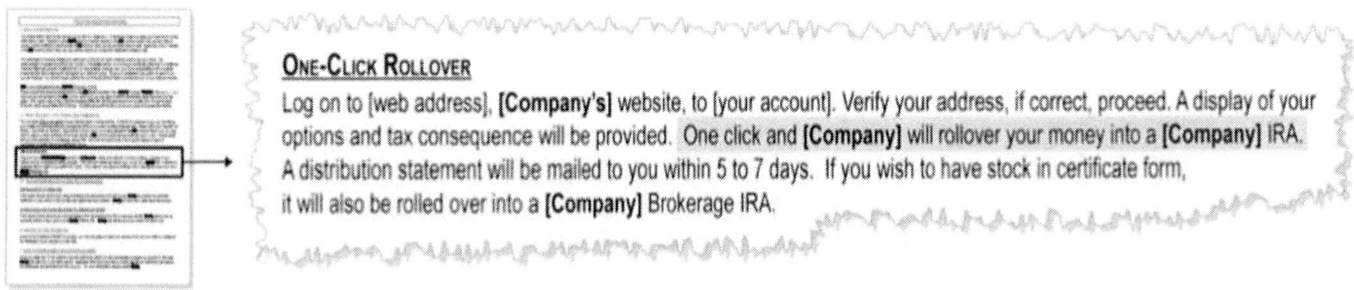

Source: Distribution materials provided to GAO by one plan sponsor.

Figure 3. One Example of a 401(k) Plan Service Provider Using Distribution Information as a Venue to Promote Their Own Retail IRA Product.

One plan provider told us that the marketing of IRA rollover products by service providers can be pervasive throughout plan documents, and even the summary plan descriptions might steer participants into a provider's retail products. Although many service providers said they do not promote their own investment products in interactions with plan participants of the plans they serve, we reviewed examples of educational materials that couple distribution information with information on the providers' retail IRA products. We also found several separation packets that emphasized the simplicity of rolling over to the service providers' IRAs, as opposed to the relative complexity of other providers' IRAs, and added flexibility regarding distributions and beneficiaries. Additionally, many of the providers that provided written responses to our questions indicated that the educational materials they give to participants include their firms' IRA products as examples. While some plan sponsors may attempt to limit such marketing activities, other sponsors are either unaware that they can negotiate a provider's ability to promote its products to plan participants or they do not have the resources to prepare their own materials in lieu of the materials offered by their providers.[59]

The marketing of IRA products by providers is not limited to written materials but may also be pervasive in other interactions with participants. Participants can be steered toward IRA rollovers when receiving information from service providers, including via call centers. We were told by industry experts that

- participants think that they have received investment advice from their service providers that is solely in the participants' best interest, even though they may not actually be receiving such advice;
- service providers use their websites and call centers, including making outbound calls to plan participants, as a means of marketing their firms' retail IRA products and steering participants into them; and
- when taking a distribution participants may be steered first into a provider's IRA product, and if they opt out or decline that rollover option, they are then directed to a portal sponsored by the same provider where participants can access other companies' IRA platforms, for which the service provider receives some compensation if a participant chooses a company's IRA through that portal.

In addition to marketing their products, service providers may offer their call center representatives financial or other incentives for asset retention, when separating plan participants leave their assets in the plan or roll over to one of the providers' IRA products, which could lead to representatives promoting the providers' products over other options. When our investigator called 30 401(k) plan service providers he found that, even though he identified himself as a potential participant in the plans served by the providers, 11 service provider representatives encouraged him to roll his plan savings to an IRA instead of to the new plan without specific knowledge of his financial circumstances. In addition, about half (16 of 30) of the representatives brought up the fact that IRAs have more investment options than 401(k) plans. Finally, some of the call center representatives did not mention the option of leaving funds in the old plan, 12 of 30 representatives raised doubts about the caller's ability to roll over to a new 401(k) plan, and several emphasized the rollover assistance they provide. See figure 4 below for excerpts from some of the conversations.

Call 1

Representative: "...it almost always makes sense to roll [the current 401(k)] into an IRA that has no fees, like a no-fee IRA, because basically, you know, even if you like the funds that are in your current 401(k), you can just buy those in your IRA. It's the same thing. Most all of those funds are available retail...when you buy when you have them in an IRA, so **you are not missing anything by rolling it over, but you are forfeiting some things by leaving it where it is."**

Call 2

Representative: **"I would go with the IRA.** It's just that it gives you a lot more flexibility and control. I mean, from an investment standpoint, it's not tied to an employer. It's in your own name. It's just a lot more advantageous in terms of not having it tied to an employer. It's in your own account."

Call 3

Representative: "It makes no difference on our end. I am just trying to let you know that, **if I were in your shoes and you are not wanting to use the money for a loan, I would head the IRA route."**

Call 4

Representative: **"...I'm a firm believer in taking control of your money and putting it into an IRA that you can control.** And that essentially takes it away from the employer's command, if you will."

Investigator: "Okay."

Representative: "So I highly recommend, in your particular situation, that **the IRA would be your best route for this."**

Source: GAO investigative calls to 401(k) plan service providers.

Figure 4. Examples of 401(k) Plan Service Providers (Who May or May Not Be Fiduciaries) Giving a Potential Plan Participant Guidance Favoring IRAs.

A short video of examples of 401(k) service providers giving a potential participant guidance favoring IRAs is available online at www.gao.gov/multimedia/

As a result of being allowed to market their IRAs and retail investment products in educational materials or in interactions with participants, providers are able to steer participants to their products without the participants clearly being aware that they are being marketed to instead of being advised about their options.

While some service providers appear to take full advantage of current regulations that allow them to market their retail IRA products and services, service providers often seek to avoid ERISA fiduciary status and, as a result, are careful not to provide assistance that could trigger fiduciary liability. Service providers told us that the regulatory environment, specifically the lack of clarity between investment education and investment advice, creates challenges for them in providing information to participants. Experts said that, to limit liability, some service providers are very cautious when interacting with plan participants and discussing distribution options for fear that the information they provide may be construed as investment advice, which would trigger ERISA fiduciary liability. One sponsor noted that the materials provided to participants are dense and contain a lot of "legalese" in order to observe the regulations that govern a sponsor's interactions with participants. In addition, plans and service providers tend to provide participants with pre-packaged materials that are generic in nature in part to avoid crossing the line from providing investment education to investment advice.

Absent adequate agency guidance about the application of the ERISA definition of fiduciary, including the types of information and assistance that constitute investment advice, which may trigger fiduciary liability, many plan sponsors and service providers are uncertain and concerned about what they can provide to plan participants. As a result, for fear of incurring added liability, plan sponsors and service providers may unnecessarily limit the education they provide to plan participants about their distribution options when separating from employment. Consequently, participants may continue to receive limited information and assistance about what to do with their 401(k) plan savings, while continuing to be susceptible to the ongoing and pervasive marketing of IRAs. By resolving its fiduciary definition initiative and requiring that service providers disclose their financial interests and the standards to which they are subject (ERISA fiduciary standards, SEC standards, or others), Labor can provide plan sponsors and service providers with a clearer understanding about the information they can provide to participants upon separation from employment and whether their assistance subjects them to ERISA fiduciary standards. Without such action, participants may remain unaware that the investment information they receive could be conflicted information, because they do not know that service providers may or may not (1) be subject to ERISA fiduciary requirements or other standards when speaking to them,[60] and (2) have direct financial interests in the investment decisions participants may make.

PARTICIPANTS FACE CHALLENGES IN MAKING ROLLOVER DECISIONS

Comparing Distribution Options Is Complex

Complex Information May Make It Difficult for Participants to Understand and Compare Distribution Options

401(k) plan participants separating from their employers may find it difficult to understand and compare their distribution options. Service providers and other experts we interviewed said that the number and complexity of factors that differ among the four main options make it difficult to understand the possible consequences of each, such as the differences in tax withholding. Participants may have difficulty finding information on IRA fees, and when they do find it, they may not understand it. Experts cite some key differences that individuals separating from an employer may want to consider when making a distribution decision, as shown in table 3. Determining what factors are most important for an individual must be done on a case-by-case basis, based on individual circumstances, capabilities, and needs.

As we have previously reported, understanding these complex factors is especially difficult given that many participants have limited financial literacy skills.[61] Studies have found that many individuals lack knowledge of even basic financial concepts.[62] Yet, as financial markets have become more complex, the proliferation of new investment products has made obtaining clear information and understanding financial concepts increasingly necessary for participants to make sound retirement investment decisions. Experts have noted that investors should consider a number of factors, including their time horizon for retirement, risk tolerance, and the value and asset allocation of other retirement savings when making investment decisions.[63] One industry-based survey found that 52 percent of the participants surveyed (which included, but was not limited to 401(k) plan participants) said they lacked sophistication about financial matters.

Table 3. Some Key Differences between 401(k) Plans and IRAs to Consider When Making Distribution Decisions

Key differences	401(k) Plan	IRA
Investment selection and monitoring	Plan fiduciaries are responsible for selecting and monitoring investment options in the best interest of the participant.	Individual is solely responsible for selecting and monitoring investments.
Investment choices	Employer-selected investment options from which to choose.	Nearly unlimited investment options from which tochoose.a
Acceptance of rollovers	May or may not accept rollovers from previous employers' 401(k) plans or other qualified accounts.	IRAs will generally accept rollovers from an employer plan or another IRA.
Fees	Plans may offer low-fee mutual fund investments through institutional pricing.b	IRA providers generally offer retail mutual funds and reserve less costly share classes for only those individuals with large balances.
Feedisclosure	Subject to Labor regulations regarding disclosure of fee information intended to make it easier for participants to understand and compare fees.	Not subject to Labor regulations regarding disclosure of fee information, but SEC requires certain disclosures in individual mutual fund prospectuses and summary prospectuses.
Fee payment	Many plans absorb the cost of administrative and other non-investment fees.b	Investor generally pays administrative costs and fees.c
Access to funds before retirement	Plans may allow non-taxable pre-retirement loans for certain reasons or hardship distributions but generally restrict distributions prior to separation.	No pre-retirement loans but taxable distributions may be taken for any reason.

Table 3. (Continued)

Key differences	401(k) Plan	IRA
Tax liabilities	Distributions taxed as income unless rolled over and, for other than direct rollovers, mandatory withholding of 20 percent of distributions for tax purposes.d	Distributions taxed as income unless rolled over,ebut no mandatory withholding of 20 percent of distribution for tax purposes.d

Source: Summary from GAO interviews of experts and GAO research of expert opinions.

[a] IRA funds used to purchase insurance or collectibles, such as antiques and stamps, are treated as distributions. 26 U.S.C. § 408(e)(5) and (m).

[b] For information about 401(k) plan fees see GAO-12-325.

[c] In addition to lowering or waiving fees for investors with large balances, IRA providers sometimes, as a rollover promotion, waive account maintenance fees.

[d] Additional tax of 10 percent may apply for distributions before age 591/2.

[e] Qualified distributions from Roth IRAs are not taxed.

The study also found that about half of "relatively engaged" investors felt confident that they knew how to select a diverse mix of investments and 40 percent said that they knew how much they should save for retirement. In contrast, less than 20 percent of "less-engaged" investors said they thought they could do these things.[64] Other research indicates that many plan participants know little about the fees that they already pay in their 401(k) plans, making it unlikely that they could compare plan fees to those of another plan or an IRA. The lack of financial education and ability to make sound financial choices may leave participants unequipped to understand and weigh the factors key to making the best decision regarding their 401(k) plan savings.

In addition, it can be difficult for individuals to get accurate information when trying to identify and understand these factors. For example, in response to a call from our investigator, a representative at a service provider's call center said that IRAs differ from 401(k) plans because an IRA "has no taxes". The representative did not explain what taxes he was referring to in his comment. Though IRA cash outs do not require up-front tax withholding the way 401(k) plan cash outs do, ultimately most IRA[65] and 401(k) plan distributions will be taxed the same way at the end of the year. Given many individuals' lack of basic financial literacy, such a statement could be misunderstood by some to mean that savings in a 401(k) plan are taxed but savings in an IRA are not. In fact, both IRAs and 401(k) plans offer a place to accumulate retirement savings tax-free until distribution.

Rollovers to IRAs Require Complex Choices, and Fees are Difficult to Identify

As shown in figure 5, an individual choosing to roll over their plan distribution into an IRA must first make several complex investment choices. These include allocating money across asset classes and choosing investments from among thousands of mutual funds and other options that offer the right balance of risk, return, and fees—which may be confusing to some investors. Moreover, the myriad investment options in an IRA make the process of comparing them more difficult than in a 401(k) plan, which may have a limited menu of investment options. For example, some service providers who offer IRAs promote their access to a "self-directed brokerage window," which allows an investor to choose from an even larger number of potential investment options and to buy and sell individual stocks and even gold without the direct assistance of a broker,[66] but this option can be associated with high fees compared to other mutual fund alternatives.

As shown in figure 6, prudent decision making regarding IRAs and the rollover process generally may require review and comprehension of a fair amount of documentation. For example, once participants have chosen to go with a particular IRA provider, the IRA application refers them to read multiple documents, including investment prospectuses, which they should review if they are interested in re-investing their retirement plan savings in an investment other than a money market account, the typical default investment for IRA rollovers. In addition, to prudently compare the many funds offered before making investment choices, an investor must then obtain and analyze additional prospectuses.

IRA fee information is especially difficult to find and, if it is located, to understand. Our review of websites of 10 large IRA providers showed that IRA fee information was generally scattered across the providers' websites in multiple documents, making it difficult to identify all applicable fees.[67] For example, in one rollover application, the schedule of fees, where an IRA provider typically lists investment fees, was located in the last section of a 49-page supplement. This section covered the fee information over four and a half pages using 8-point typeface (this size). In fact, fees are often located in footnotes with small typeface in the documents given to IRA investors. As shown in figure 7, even the word "fee" can be hard to find for IRA rollover customers and investors.

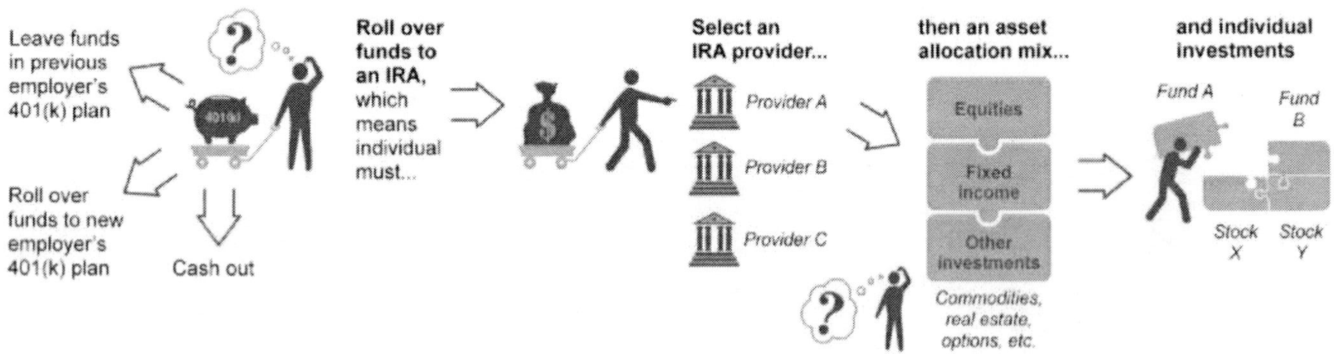

Source: GAO analysis.

Figure 5. IRA Rollover Decisions Involve Several Complex Investment Choices.

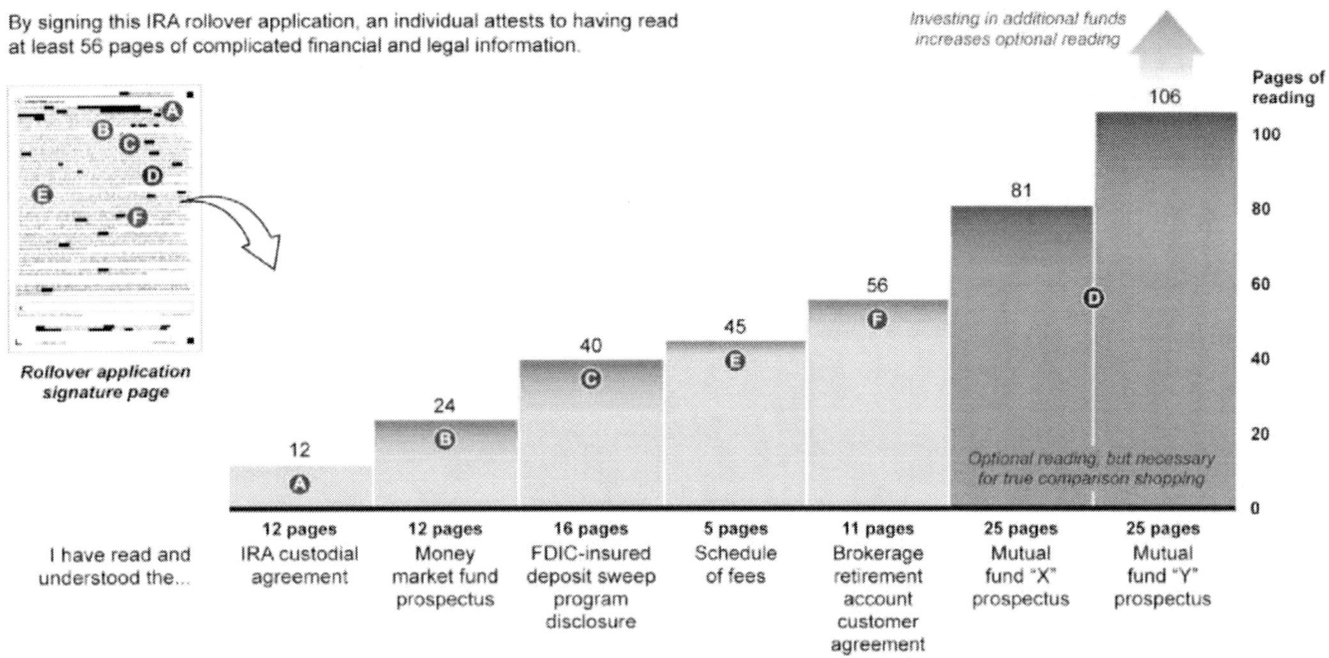

Source: GAO analysis of the IRA rollover application used by one of the largest IRA providers.

Note: Mutual funds X and Y are examples based on the prospectus for one of the most popular target date funds. Actual number of pages could differ depending on specific funds reviewed.

Figure 6. Number of Pages in One IRA Rollover Application and Associated Investment Research.

Source: GAO analysis of financial documents using a word cloud generator at: www.wordle.net.

Note: A "word cloud" shows the words used most in the document. The more often a word appeared, the larger it is shown. See appendix I for more information about how this figure was created.

Figure 7. The Most Frequently Used Words in One IRA Rollover Application and Target Date Fund Prospectus.

Once an individual obtains IRA fee information, it can be difficult to understand. Labor's recent fee disclosure regulations[68] require 401(k) plans to disclose plan fees with greater clarity than IRA providers, which have no such requirement, are likely to provide investors.[69] For instance, plan disclosures generally list the different 401(k) plan investment options' costs side by side to facilitate comparison, whereas IRA disclosures will typically not have fee data with comparable clarity and presentation.[70] One plan provider told us that it would help investors understand the differences between their 401(k) plans and IRAs if IRA providers were required to provide the same level of fee disclosure.

Complex fee structures also make IRA fee information difficult to understand. Specifically, the number and variety of IRA investments introduce different types of fees that may be unfamiliar to participants and are not easy to understand. For example, brokerage fees for an IRA investor vary depending on many factors, including investor choices about how often to buy or sell an asset; whether to make transactions over the phone, internet, or with assistance from a representative; buying domestic or foreign stock; and how long to hold an asset. In addition, industry research shows that many investors want advice and help investing their retirement savings, which are services that can further add to the cost of investing in an IRA. For example, investment management or investment advisory fees are typically a percentage of assets under management. At one of the largest IRA providers, the annual advisory fee is 1.5 percent of assets for balances up to $500,000, with rates decreasing for larger accounts.

Finally, misleading statements also make it difficult to understand IRA fees. Calls made by our investigator to 401(k) plan service providers, most of which offer IRA products, found that 7 of 30 call center representatives (representing firms administering at least 34 percent of IRA assets at the end of the 1st quarter in 2011) said that their IRAs were "free" or had no fees with a minimum balance, without clearly explaining that investment, transaction, and other fees could still apply, depending on investment decisions.[71] In our review of 10 IRA websites, we found 5 providers that made similar claims, often with certain conditions such as a $50,000 minimum balance or consent to receive electronic statements explained separately in footnotes.[72] For example, an IRA provider's website we reviewed stated that the provider would waive annual custodial fees if the balance exceeded an unspecified amount and only referred vaguely to other fees that might still apply, which were disclosed in multiple separate documents available upon request. Accurate information on when IRA providers will waive fees and what fees they will waive can be difficult for participants both to locate and understand.

Rollovers to New 401(k) Plans May Prove Difficult without Complete Information

Participants thinking of rolling their plan savings to a plan offered by a new employer have to first compare the terms and investment opportunities laid out by the new plan sponsor to see if that plan offers better terms, given their investment goals, than either the old plan, if remaining in the plan is an option, or an IRA. Currently, plan sponsors have considerable flexibility with respect to plan design, including participant requirements, distribution options, and access to loans. 73 In reviewing the new plan, participants may find that it does not accept rollover balances from other 401(k) plans. Our investigator's calls to 30 401(k) plan service providers found that several call center representatives also warned that the caller's potential new 401(k) plan, serviced by their firm, might restrict or prohibit rollovers from other 401(k) plans. Even when plans accept rollovers from other plans, industry experts we interviewed told us that plan sponsors do not have strong incentives to accept the assets of new participants and may not promote the option. As a result, given the effort participants must make to understand new plans' rules and the lack of encouragement from plan sponsors and others to roll over balances into new plans, participants may remain unaware of their ability to roll over into new plans or may be unmotivated to exercise that option.

Service providers told us that they want to retain assets of participants separating from plans they serve. As a result, they may encourage participants to roll over distributions into their IRA products and never mention or even discourage plan participants from rolling their distributions into new plans with different service providers. Marketing and research firms also cite active contact as one strategy providers should employ to retain assets. Experts specifically cited the practice of making outbound calls to participants as part of asset retention strategies and also noted that providers often only target participants with larger balances. Consequently, participants are likely to receive targeted information about rolling over into an IRA but may receive little information about rollover options outside of their current providers' IRAs. Service providers also told us that they seek to capture assets moving out of plans serviced by other providers. During our investigator's calls, about a third of call center representatives of 401(k) plan service providers encouraged the caller to roll over 401(k) plan savings from the exemployer's plan to the service provider's IRA products, and 12 did not mention the option to leave money in the current plan. However, of the 18 who did mention the option to stay in the plan, 5 did so only after being asked about it by the caller.

Plans May Encourage Separating Participants Not to Keep Savings in the Plan

Currently, plans may treat participants who are employees and those no longer employed by the plan sponsor differently. Surveys of plan sponsors and asset managers for plans suggest that roughly 60 percent of plans are ambivalent about or even averse to keeping participants savings in the plan after they separate from employment.[74] Service providers and experts corroborated these findings, telling us that some plan sponsors do not want to retain separated employees' savings in their plans for a variety of reasons, such as reducing administrative burdens, costs, and legal liability.[75] These attitudes are evident in some plans' practice of treating active and separated participants differently,[76] making a former employer's plan a less favorable place for the separated participant to leave their account balance. For example, some plans:

- Charge higher or additional fees to separated participants. One service provider we interviewed said that plan sponsors commonly charge an added administrative fee to the accounts of separated participants, making the plan more expensive than other options, like rolling over the account balance to a new plan or an IRA.[77]

- Restrict the separated participants' ability to manage their savings in the plan, including their ability to take a loan.
- Discourage separated participants, perhaps inadvertently, from leaving their savings in plans by limiting their distribution options. For example, it is not uncommon for plans to limit distributions to the total balance rather than allowing partial distributions, which encourages some participants to move all their money out of a plan, providing a disincentive for someone with a sizeable balance or nearing the age for required minimum distribution to leave their savings in their plan.[78]

Indirect Rollovers from 401(k) Plans Have Tax Consequences

Example of tax consequences for an indirect rollover from a 401(k) plan

Jane Doe separates from her employer and, not wanting to leave her 401(k) savings in the employer's plan while she decides what to do with it, she cashes out her $50,000 balance. Jane receives a check payable to her for just $40,000 because the IRS requires a mandatory withholding of 20 percent ($10,000 in this case) for distributions; the amount that could be owed in taxes if she does not reinvest the money in a tax-qualified account, like a new 401(k) or an IRA.

However, after a month, she picks an IRA provider and reinvests her $40,000. Because she reinvests her distributions within the 60-day grace period for indirect rollovers, the $40,000 she reinvested is not taxed.

But unless Jane comes up with the $10,000 in distributions that was withheld for the IRS, and also invests that amount in a tax-qualified account within the 60-day period, the IRS will treat the $10,000 as a cash-out and assess income tax.

Since Jane is younger than 59½, the IRS will also assess an additional early-withdrawal tax of 10 percent ($1,000 in this case) and, depending on her tax bracket, return $9,000 or less to her.

Although information about the tax consequences of taking a distribution from a 401(k) plan is one area where disclosure is required for plan participants, industry experts told us that the information often comes too late to inform the decision and is too complex for most people to understand. Participants separating from an employer may not understand the tax consequences of receiving a cash out from their 401(k) plan, which can be especially confusing if the distribution is rolled over into a qualified employer plan or IRA within 60 days; such a transaction is deemed an indirect rollover.[79]

In 2010, IRS revised its standard notice regarding tax information that plans are required to provide participants. Three service providers and one service provider trade association told us that notice helps to educate participants about their distribution options. However, many experts we spoke to still believe that participants may find it difficult to understand that certain types of distributions have different tax consequences, because the tax information they get from their plans is complex. For example, one plan provider told us that many participants do not understand the difference between direct and indirect rollovers.

A misunderstanding of these options could prove costly for a participant, however, given the different tax treatment of the two methods of rolling over plan savings. Money transferred through a direct rollover—that is, made payable from one 401(k) plan directly to another qualified employer plan or an IRA—is not considered income and, therefore, does not have tax consequences.

However, an indirect rollover from a plan (when a distribution is made by a check payable to the participant, who then rolls the money into another eligible plan or IRA within 60 days) requires mandatory withholding for tax purposes. Specifically, when a participant receives a cash out, the 401(k) plan must withhold 20 percent of the distribution for tax purposes. If the individual rolls the remaining 80 percent into a tax-qualified account within the 60- day grace period (an indirect rollover) the individual will have to add funds from other sources to replace the 20 percent withheld or that withholding will count as income subject to income tax. (See the side bar for an example of the tax consequences of an indirect rollover from a 401(k) plan.) In contrast, indirect rollovers or cash outs of savings from IRAs, though also subject to any applicable taxes at year end, are not subject to mandatory withholding at the time of distribution.

Finally, distributions from either 401(k) plans or IRAs taken before an individual reaches age $59^1/_2$ are subject to an additional 10 percent tax, though specific requirements differ for 401(k) plans and IRAs.[80]

Information Participants Receive May Not Clearly Explain Distribution Options or Be Provided in a Timely Manner

Currently, federal regulations do not ensure that plans provide complete and timely information on distribution options to plan participants when they separate from employment. IRS requires plans to provide participants:

1) information that describes the tax consequences of the different distribution options (often referred to as the "402(f) special tax notice"),[81] and
2) information about a participant's right to defer receipt of distribution.[82]

The 402(f) special tax notice addresses the tax consequences of distributions as well as some general information about rollovers. However, it does not provide a full discussion of all the options that may be available to separating participants or touch on other important factors participants should consider in making a distribution decision. For instance, as shown in appendix II, Treasury's model 402(f) special tax notice does not include any discussion of leaving funds in a plan.

The IRS published a proposed rule in 2008 to expand on the information requirements for the second of the two required notices.[83] Specifically, under the proposed regulation plans would be required to include in the information provided, among other things, statements that:

> "some currently available investment options in the plan may not be generally available on similar terms outside the plan and contact information for obtaining additional information on the general availability outside the plan of currently available investment options in the plan."
>
> and
>
> "fees and expenses (including administrative or investment-related fees) outside the plan may be different from fees and expenses that apply to the participant's account and contact information for obtaining information on such fees."

However, there was no requirement that plans explicitly disclose that IRAs may have higher fees than investments in a plan. Given recent research showing participants' lack of knowledge about their plans' fees, participants may also not understand that plans often offer investments at lower cost than the typical retail fees charged by IRAs.

Additionally, in light of the marketing efforts of IRA providers –which our website review found can include claims that IRAs are "free"—as well as the recent spotlight on 401(k) plan fees, highlighted by Labor's new fee disclosure requirements, simply stating that fees and expenses could be "different" may not be sufficient. Such statements may not clearly convey to participants that they could pay more for investments outside of a plan or the long-term effect of higher fees on their retirement plan savings.

Moreover, IRS regulations do not require plans to provide the requisite distribution information when a participant is separating from employment with the plan sponsor; rather, the information is required within a specified window of time prior to receipt of a distribution. We identified no current legislative or regulatory requirements ensuring that participants receive timely information on their distribution options before they have made a decision to take a distribution. There are also no requirements for plans to give participants comprehensive or balanced information comparing their options at the time of job separation.

In lieu of regulations from IRS or Labor, experts told us that plans and their providers determine when participants receive such information. Although some service providers we interviewed said that they typically send separation packets as soon as participants separate from employment, since there is no requirement to provide a detailed packet at separation, participants cannot rely on getting the information they need in time to make a distribution decision. In fact, several service providers we spoke to said they do not provide information until the participant requests a distribution.

Many experts we interviewed said participants are also in need of concise and clear information on their rollover options. Information that plans and service providers give participants can be either too generic and without detail, leaving participants without an understanding of the key factors they need to know to make decisions about their savings, or too long and technical, leaving participants overwhelmed and confused.

Several service providers told us that the limited scope of the information provided may not clearly inform participants of their options, including the option to keep funds in the current plan or to roll over to a new employer plan. About a fifth (14 out of 76) of the 401(k) plan sponsors who responded to our survey noted that they do not provide or do not know if they provide their participants with information about the option to roll over funds, upon separation, to plans with other employers.[84]

Without more complete, clear, and timely information on their distribution options, participants separating from employers will continue to be at risk of making ill-informed decisions and may choose the administratively easier and more promoted route of rolling into an IRA instead of choosing other options that may be more beneficial. Providing a document that clearly lays out each of the four basic options a separating plan participant has puts the participant in a better position to determine the option that is in his or her best interest.

The document could list factors beyond tax implications that experts said that participants should consider and could reference detailed information (for example, lists of questions consumers should ask investment professionals about fees, conflicts of interest, and standards of conduct). Among several factors highlighted in table 3 above, which lists some key differences between 401(k) plans and IRAs to consider when deciding whether to stay in a 401(k) plan or roll over funds into an IRA, some experts specifically highlighted that fees may be lower in plans than in retail IRAs (especially when retail brokerage fees are factored in), that fee disclosure requirements make 401(k) plan fees easier to identify than IRA fees, and that the fiduciary duties of a plan sponsor to a plan participant differ from those of an IRA investment adviser to a retail customer.

By law, Labor is charged with maintaining an outreach program to promote retirement income savings,[85] including the creation of educational materials describing basic concepts related to retirement savings, and Labor provides such information for plan participants on its website. Additionally, Labor officials told us that the agency also disseminates some information through industry-based organizations.

However, according to Labor officials, Labor does not reach out to plan sponsors to ensure that they give plan participants needed educational information specific to distribution options, nor does Labor reach out to plan participants directly. As a result, plan participants may not be aware of, or receive, Labor's educational materials. Our review of Labor's website found that there is valuable information on retirement plans for plan participants. However, since the information is not directly provided to them, plan participants would have to know about the website and know what to look for in order to find information on their distribution options.[86]

CONCLUSION

Participants of 401(k) plans make decisions to stay within the plan environment or roll over into IRAs based on the information available to them and the time and energy they have to take action. Unfortunately, the effort they have to make to understand their options and pursue a course of action can be daunting. As a result, participants can be easily steered towards IRAs given the number of administrative obstacles and disincentives to staying in the plan environment and the pervasive marketing of IRAs by 401(k) service providers and IRA providers generally.

Rolling over to an IRA can be a reasonable choice for many participants and, given the amount of money in IRAs, many individuals and former 401(k) plan participants appear satisfied with that option. But other options, such as staying in their current plan or rolling over into their new employers' plans, may also be viable alternatives and could even be better options depending on an individual's unique circumstances.

Currently, sponsors' policies governing the accounts of separated participants and the processing of rollovers may serve as disincentives to staying in a plan or rolling assets to a new employer plan. In addition, sponsors' practice regarding the process of accepting money from other plans can also create disincentives.

Plan sponsors' caution and confusion about IRS policies regarding the consequences of inadvertently accepting funds from non-qualified plans is especially puzzling given the agency's clear guidance stating that a plan will not be at risk of losing its qualified status if it reasonably concluded that the distributing plan was qualified.

By working together to disseminate and clarify guidance, Labor and IRS can make it easier for plans to accept rollovers into their plans and can help ensure that each tax-preferred vehicle available to participants is easily accessible for them, enabling distribution decisions to be based on what best meets participants' financial needs rather than on which tax deferred vehicle is easiest to roll into.

Finally, the practice of sending direct-rollover checks to participants appears archaic when communications are increasingly conducted electronically. Restricting this practice can help participants avoid losing track of their retirement plan savings due to a misstep on their part, and can help shorten the time needed to complete a rollover and make plan-to-plan rollovers more efficient for everyone involved.

Our work has also demonstrated that 401(k) plan participants separating from their employers need help to obtain and understand information about the four distribution options and IRA products being marketed to them by providers. Providing information to participants about their options that is clear and in plain English, and easily understood and comparable, at a time when a participant is thinking about taking action with their retirement savings could be helpful.

Requiring a summary document that explains to participants what their distribution options are, what factors they should consider when thinking about those options, and steps they can take at the time they are considering their decisions, can help participants better understand what to do when changing jobs or retiring. Better information is obviously an important step in helping participants make decisions, although improving basic financial literacy in general, which includes helping participants understand fundamental concepts such as investing, is another important component that can help participants make important decisions to secure their retirement.

Additionally, although Labor has attempted to help plan participants understand the information they are given from providers, current requirements do not sufficiently assist participants in understanding the financial interests that service providers have in the distribution and investment decisions that participants make, nor sufficiently clarify the fiduciary responsibility that providers may have when providing assistance to participants who are in need of guidance. Requiring service providers to clearly disclose their financial interests in participants' decisions and the extent of their fiduciary obligations can also help participants better understand providers' roles and assess the guidance or information received from them. Moreover, resolving the uncertainty plans and providers face regarding activities that trigger fiduciary liability may help service providers provide better information to participants regarding their distribution options and assist them in making more informed decisions about their retirement savings.

Finally, Treasury has proposed regulations that would require a notice be provided to participants separating from their employer explaining the consequences of taking their money out of their 401(k) plan. The notice would specifically explain that investment options offered in a plan may not be available outside of a plan for the same cost. We previously recommended that the Secretary of the Treasury amend the applicable requirements of the department's proposed disclosure rule to specifically require that service providers, when recommending the purchase of investment products outside retirement plans, inform plan participants that fees applicable outside their plans may be higher than fees applicable within their plans. Requiring that such a notice be provided to participants upon separation from their employer can help participants better understand that plans often offer investments at lower costs than can be found in retail investments, such as those in IRAs.

Recommendations for Executive Action

We are making 5 recommendations based on our review.

To help reduce obstacles and disincentives to keeping retirement savings in the 401(k) plan environment, we recommend that the Commissioner of Internal Revenue and Secretary of Labor review policies that affect separating employees leaving retirement savings in an employer's plan and, for those who choose to roll their distributions into another 401(k) plan, the process of plan-to-plan rollovers. As part of such a review,

- The Commissioner of Internal Revenue and the Secretary of Labor should review the lack of standardization of sponsor practices related to plan-to-plan rollovers and of policies affecting participants who leave plan savings in a former employer's plan, with the aim of taking any regulatory action they deem appropriate. Such action could address obstacles like sponsors refusing to accept rollovers from other plans, and disincentives like plans restricting participants' control over savings once they separate from the employer, and charging different fees for inactive participants.
- The Commissioner of Internal Revenue and the Secretary of Labor should work together to communicate to plan sponsors IRS's guidance on the relief from tax disqualification provided for plans that accept rollovers later determined to have come from a plan that was not tax qualified.

  In helping to better disseminate IRS's guidance to plan sponsors, Labor may also provide feedback to IRS to help ensure that the guidance is clear and understandable, so that it adequately addresses plan sponsors' concerns about their own plans' qualified status and helps reduce delays in processing rollovers from other plans.

- The Commissioner of Internal Revenue should revise rules that allow plans and providers to send direct-rollover distribution checks to individuals rather than to the receiving entities to which the checks are written.

To help ensure that when plan participants separate from an employer and are deciding what to do with their retirement plan savings they receive adequate, timely, and balanced information, we recommend that the Secretary of Labor take the following actions:

- Develop a concise written summary explaining a participant's four distribution options and listing key factors a participant should consider when comparing possible investments, and require sponsors to provide that summary to a participant upon separation from an employer. Should Labor conclude that additional statutory authority is needed to take this action, it should seek that authority from the Congress.
- Finalize the agency's initiative to clarify the ERISA definition of fiduciary, and, in doing so, require plan service providers, when assisting participants with distribution options, to disclose any financial interests they may have in the outcome of those decisions in a clear, consistent, and prominent manner; the conditions under which they are subject to any regulatory standards (such as ERISA fiduciary standards, SEC standards, or others) and what those standards mean for the participant.

AGENCY COMMENTS AND OUR EVALUATION

We provided a draft of this report to the Department of Labor, Department of the Treasury, Internal Revenue Service, and the Consumer Financial Protection Bureau for review. Labor, Treasury, and IRS provided technical comments, which we have incorporated where appropriate. Labor and Treasury also provided written comments. The Consumer Financial Protection Bureau did not have any comments.

GAO Response to Labor Comments

As stated in its letter, Labor believes its work regarding the definition of a fiduciary is key to addressing much of the concern raised in our report. We agree with Labor that a clearer understanding of when persons providing advice are subject to ERISA's fiduciary standards will help to protect participants from conflicts of interest and self-dealing. Labor stated that a new proposed rule will be issued in 2013 addressing the circumstances under which a person is considered to be a "fiduciary" by reason of giving investment advice to an employee benefit plan or a plan's participants. Labor also commented on our report section addressing these issues and noted that when advisers make specific recommendations to invest in particular investment products, it is critical that they adhere to ERISA's fiduciary standards, particularly where conflicts of interest may exist. We agree with Labor's conclusion that adherence to ERISA fiduciary standards is an important element in protecting plans and participants. Additionally, while we had previously pointed out that providers reluctant to become fiduciaries may limit the availability of investment advice as well as education to participants, we revised the section to better convey that upcoming clarification about the definition of a fiduciary, and about what constitutes investment advice and education, will help plan sponsors and providers understand what they can give to participants in different circumstances and should mitigate their concerns about assisting plan participants.

Overall, Labor generally agreed with our recommendations and will explore ways to implement them. Specifically, regarding our recommendation to develop a concise summary document explaining separating participants' distribution options and require plan sponsors to disseminate the document to plan participants, Labor noted it will address the recommendation by evaluating its regulatory approaches within the constraints of its existing statutory authority. While ERISA does not grant Labor specific authority to require plan sponsors to provide such information, it does grant Labor broad authority regarding protection of participant benefits and the duties of plan fiduciaries. In response to Labor's comment on this specific recommendation, we have added language indicating that should Labor conclude that additional statutory authority is needed, it should seek that authority from the Congress.

Regarding our recommendation to require service providers to disclose any financial interests they may have in a participant's decisions and whether their assistance is subject to any standards as part of revising the interpretive bulletin on investment education, Labor commented that such activities should be part of the department's efforts to amend the regulatory definition of fiduciary. Labor noted that because the current regulation addresses the circumstances under which a person becomes a fiduciary by reason of rendering investment advice for a fee, any proposed changes to that regulation could affect the types of information treated as non-fiduciary investment education under the interpretive bulletin. We concur with Labor's assessment and revised our recommendations accordingly.

With regard to our recommendation that the department review the lack of standardization among plans regarding plan-to-plan rollovers and participants leaving their savings in former employers' plans, Labor noted that such plan design features historically have not been viewed as subject to Labor's regulatory authority under Title I of ERISA, but have been subject to IRS oversight. As a result of Labor's comments, we revised the recommendation to include the Commissioner of Internal Revenue. However, Labor noted that it would evaluate whether it has available regulatory approaches to address the recommendation. Given Labor's broad oversight authority of plans and plan sponsors, we continue to believe that Labor is essential to addressing this recommendation in coordination with IRS.

Regarding our recommendation that Labor and IRS work together to ensure that plan sponsors are fully informed about IRS' rules regarding plans' acceptance of rollovers that are later determined to have come from a non-qualified plan, Labor questioned the appropriateness of being included in the recommendation inasmuch as the interpretation of the IRC's tax-qualification provisions related to acceptance of rollovers is not within Labor's jurisdiction. Our recommendation focuses on IRS rules and guidance. However, given Labor's broad oversight authority with respect to employer-sponsored plans, it is important that Labor help ensure that plan sponsors are aware of and understand IRS' guidance. Therefore, we agree with Labor that it should assist IRS in its outreach efforts and suggest ways that newly issued guidance could be more clearly communicated to plan sponsors. To better clarify our intent for Labor's role, we revised the recommendation to clearly convey that Labor's role should be more centered on communication and outreach to plan sponsors.

GAO Response to Treasury Comments

Treasury generally agreed with our recommendations and in its letter noted that the department and IRS can take steps to improve the rollover process so that more plan participants will be able to more easily roll over retirement assets to the their current employer's retirement plan. Specifically, with regard to our recommendation that IRS and Labor work together to disseminate guidance for plan sponsors on the relief from disqualification when plans accept rollovers later determined to have come from a plan that is not qualified, Treasury noted that it will work to include our recommendation in its ongoing work to provide guidance facilitating rollovers into retirement plans.

Regarding our recommendation that IRS and Labor review the lack of standardization of plan-to-plan rollovers and participants leaving their savings in former employers' plans, Treasury agreed that it is important that former employees be allowed to retain their savings in a former employer's plan and described related actions the department has already taken. However, Treasury commented that it is not aware of any statutory basis for imposing a requirement that plans accept rollovers. Our recommendation makes clear that Treasury and Labor should review the lack of standardization of plan policies and practices related to planto-plan rollovers and leaving savings in a former employer's plan with the aim of taking action within each agency's purview. Doing so will help to reduce the obstacles and disincentives that plan sponsors may have and participants face related to plan-to-plan rollovers or leaving savings in a participant's current plan. Policies and practices that may create obstacles and disincentives are not limited to a sponsor's refusal to accept rollovers from other plans.

Finally, we recommended that the IRS revise rules that allow plans and providers to send direct rollover distribution checks to individuals rather than to the receiving entities to which the checks are written. We continue to believe that this is an action that needs to be taken, and in fact, some plans already process direct rollovers electronically. Addressing this issue can help to reduce unnecessary administrative obstacles for plan participants. Thus, IRS has a key role in helping to facilitate and encourage use of this practice.

Charles A. Jeszeck,
Director Education, Workforce, and Income Security Issues

APPENDIX I: OBJECTIVES, SCOPE, AND METHODOLOGY

During our review, our objectives were to identify some of the challenges plan participants separating from their employers may face (1) implementing a rollover, including plan-to-plan rollovers; (2) getting accurate and clear information about which distribution option to choose for their 401(k) plan retirement plan savings; and (3) understanding their distribution options. To answer these questions we undertook several different approaches.

To understand the rollover marketplace, we reviewed research and data from a variety of academic and industry-based sources. To understand the extent of laws and regulations on the rollover process we reviewed federal laws and regulations pertaining to 401(k) plans and IRAs, and met with government officials from the Department of Labor, the Department of the Treasury, the Internal Revenue Service, and the Consumer Financial Protection Bureau to understand their perspectives on relevant legal issues. The effect of existing laws and regulations on the rollover process was also a focus of our interviews with 401(k) plan service providers and 401(k) plan sponsors. To understand the role of 401(k) plan service providers in participants' decision-making processes when they separate from plans, we conducted structured interviews with 401(k) plan service providers. We solicited input through 29 interviews, including the largest service providers, in terms of assets under management. During our interviews we requested samples of information provided to participants. We received sample materials from 8 interviewees and we reviewed them for size and content. In addition, with the help of The SPARK Institute, Insured Retirement Institute, and Securities Industry and Financial Markets Association, which are all industry-based membership organizations, we collected written responses to questions used in our interviews from 25 service providers that offer a range of services, including recordkeeping, rollover processing, participant education, and individual IRA products.

To understand 401(k) plan sponsors' perspectives on the rollover process and the role of plans and their service providers in the rollover decision and process, we conducted a nongeneralizable survey facilitated through two member organizations, PLANSPONSOR and the Society for Human Resource Management. We received a total of 76 responses to our survey and we also interviewed 5 plan sponsors. Of the 5 plan sponsors interviewed, 2 represented small plans, 2 represented medium-sized plans, and one represented a large plan.[1] Our survey outreach was broad; PLANSPONSOR included information on our study in an e-mail that was sent to approximately 67,000 of its members and the Society for Human Resource Management sent an e-mail to 1,012 of its members. Through the survey we asked how information is provided to separating plan participants, who provides the information, the content and format of information, and the role of sponsors and service providers. To further understand what information sponsors and service providers give to participants when they separate from employment, we also requested that sponsors responding to the survey and participating in interviews with us provide samples of the information they provide. We received sample materials from 5 survey respondents and 2 interviewees and we reviewed them for size and content.

To further understand factors affecting participants' decision making when they separate from an employer, we reviewed data and reports from several industry sources.

We obtained and reviewed survey data from an industry consulting company, Spectrem Group. This company conducted a survey of individuals who had the opportunity to roll over a plan balance from a qualified employer plan within the prior 2 years. The survey was designed to, among other things, identify preferences and sources of information for those making rollover decisions. The survey data were not generalizable, according to GAO standards for statistical reliability, and statements made describing those data reflect only the experience of the 940 individuals who responded to Spectrem Group's survey. The available methodological documentation does not allow us to fully assess the quality or reliability of the survey data.

For this reason, we cannot assess how accurate or precise the estimates are and readers should be cautious in drawing conclusions about how the population of individuals eligible to roll over would act. We also obtained and reviewed industry reports from the Financial Research Corporation, Cogent Research, and Cerulli Associates.

To assess the content and availability of information available to individuals, we reviewed 10 IRA providers' websites for account fees and rollover promotions.

The providers were chosen based on the largest providers in terms of IRA assets under management, largest share of rollover assets, and largest retirement plan asset managers. To develop figure 6, we selected the IRA rollover application for one of the largest IRA providers, in terms of assets under management, and counted the pages contained in all the separate documents listed on the signature page of the application, where an applicant is told they should read and understand those documents. That page indicates that the applicant should read the prospectus for any investment they might want to make outside the default money market fund.

To reflect what reading might be required to review a separate investment, we counted the pages in one target date fund offered by the same IRA provider and counted the pages common to the target date fund family of funds regardless of target year, such as Shareholder Information. We chose a target date fund, because it is a likely choice for an investor seeking to simplify their investment decisions while achieving a mix of equity and fixed income assets. To develop figure 7, we used text from an IRA rollover application as well as the prospectus for a target date fund, which is a likely choice for investors seeking to simplify their investment decisions while achieving a mix of equity and fixed income assets, deleted proprietary names, and input the text in the word cloud generator at www.wordle.net.

The website eliminates numbers and commonly used words like "a" and "the". We also investigated the guidance and information 401(k) plan service providers give to individuals who call them. To do this, our investigative unit placed calls to 30 401(k) plan service providers, including those with the largest 401(k) plan assets under management and 27 of which also offer IRAs, including the largest IRA providers. Our undercover caller asked about rollover options and IRA costs.[2] The caller said he was starting a new job at a company that uses the company he called to administer its 401(k) plan and he wanted information about what his different options were for his savings at his old plan. He asked about pros and cons for different options, the rollover process, and investment options and fees. We established an e-mail account to which several providers sent follow-up emails and supplementary information. The recordings of the calls were transcribed by a professional service outside GAO.

We also reviewed financial literacy literature and interviewed financial advisers and other experts to better understand the challenges faced by participants regarding distribution options and decisions.

We conducted this performance audit from May 2011 to March 2013 in accordance with generally accepted government auditing standards. Those standards require that we plan and perform the audit to obtain sufficient, appropriate evidence to provide a reasonable basis for our findings and conclusions based on our audit objectives.

We believe that the evidence obtained provides a reasonable basis for findings and conclusions based on our audit objectives. We conducted our related investigative work in accordance with standards prescribed by the Council of Inspectors General on Integrity and Efficiency.

APPENDIX II: IRS MODEL 402(F) SPECIAL TAX NOTICE

For Payments Not From a
Designated Roth Account

YOUR ROLLOVER OPTIONS

You are receiving this notice because all or a portion of a payment you are receiving from the [INSERT NAME OF PLAN] (the "Plan") is eligible to be rolled over to an IRA or an employer plan. This notice is intended to help you decide whether to do such a rollover.

This notice describes the rollover rules that apply to payments from the Plan that are not from a designated Roth account (a type of account with special tax rules in some employer plans). If you also receive a payment from a designated Roth account in the Plan, you will be provided a different notice for that payment, and the Plan administrator or the payor will tell you the amount that is being paid from each account.

Rules that apply to most payments from a plan are described in the "General Information About Rollovers" section. Special rules that only apply in certain circumstances are described in the "Special Rules and Options" section.

GENERAL INFORMATION ABOUT ROLLOVERS

How can a rollover affect my taxes?

You will be taxed on a payment from the Plan if you do not roll it over. If you are under age 59½ and do not do a rollover, you will also have to pay a 10% additional income tax on early distributions (unless an exception applies). However, if you do a rollover, you will not have to pay tax until you receive payments later and the 10% additional income tax will not apply if those payments are made after you are age 59½ (or if an exception applies).

Where may I roll over the payment?

You may roll over the payment to either an IRA (an individual retirement account or individual retirement annuity) or an employer plan (a tax-qualified plan, section 403(b) plan, or governmental section 457(b) plan) that will accept the rollover. The rules of the IRA or employer plan that holds the rollover will determine your investment options, fees, and rights to payment from the IRA or employer plan (for example, no spousal consent rules apply to IRAs and IRAs may not provide loans). Further, the amount rolled over will become subject to the tax rules that apply to the IRA or employer plan.

How do I do a rollover?

There are two ways to do a rollover. You can do either a direct rollover or a 60-day rollover.

If you do a direct rollover, the Plan will make the payment directly to your IRA or an employer plan. You should contact the IRA sponsor or the administrator of the employer plan for information on how to do a direct rollover.

If you do not do a direct rollover, you may still do a rollover by making a deposit into an IRA or eligible employer plan that will accept it. You will have 60 days after you receive the payment to make the deposit. If you do not do a direct rollover, the Plan is required to withhold 20% of the payment for federal income taxes (up to the amount of cash and property received other than employer stock). This means that, in order to roll over the entire payment in a 60-day rollover, you must use other funds to make up for the 20% withheld. If you do not roll over the entire amount of the payment, the portion not rolled over will be taxed and will be subject to the 10% additional income tax on early distributions if you are under age 59½ (unless an exception applies).

How much may I roll over?

If you wish to do a rollover, you may roll over all or part of the amount eligible for rollover. Any payment from the Plan is eligible for rollover, except:

- Certain payments spread over a period of at least 10 years or over your life or life expectancy (or the lives or joint life expectancy of you and your beneficiary)
- Required minimum distributions after age 70½ (or after death)
- Hardship distributions
- ESOP dividends
- Corrective distributions of contributions that exceed tax law limitations
- Loans treated as deemed distributions (for example, loans in default due to missed payments before your employment ends)
- Cost of life insurance paid by the Plan
- Contributions made under special automatic enrollment rules that are withdrawn pursuant to your request within 90 days of enrollment
- Amounts treated as distributed because of a prohibited allocation of S corporation stock under an ESOP (also, there will generally be adverse tax consequences if you roll over a distribution of S corporation stock to an IRA).

The Plan administrator or the payor can tell you what portion of a payment is eligible for rollover.

If I don't do a rollover, will I have to pay the 10% additional income tax on early distributions?

If you are under age 59½, you will have to pay the 10% additional income tax on early distributions for any payment from the Plan (including amounts withheld for income tax) that you do not roll over, unless one of the exceptions listed below applies. This tax is in addition to the regular income tax on the payment not rolled over.

The 10% additional income tax does not apply to the following payments from the Plan:

- Payments made after you separate from service if you will be at least age 55 in the year of the separation
- Payments that start after you separate from service if paid at least annually in equal or close to equal amounts over your life or life expectancy (or the lives or joint life expectancy of you and your beneficiary)
- Payments from a governmental defined benefit pension plan made after you separate from service if you are a public safety employee and you are at least age 50 in the year of the separation
- Payments made due to disability
- Payments after your death
- Payments of ESOP dividends
- Corrective distributions of contributions that exceed tax law limitations
- Cost of life insurance paid by the Plan
- Contributions made under special automatic enrollment rules that are withdrawn pursuant to your request within 90 days of enrollment
- Payments made directly to the government to satisfy a federal tax levy
- Payments made under a qualified domestic relations order (QDRO)
- Payments up to the amount of your deductible medical expenses
- Certain payments made while you are on active duty if you were a member of a reserve component called to duty after September 11, 2001 for more than 179 days
- Payments of certain automatic enrollment contributions requested to be withdrawn within 90 days of the first contribution.

If I do a rollover to an IRA, will the 10% additional income tax apply to early distributions from the IRA?

If you receive a payment from an IRA when you are under age 59½, you will have to pay the 10% additional income tax on early distributions from the IRA, unless an exception applies. In general, the exceptions to the 10% additional income tax for early distributions from an IRA are the same as the exceptions listed above for early distributions from a plan. However, there are a few differences for payments from an IRA, including:

- There is no exception for payments after separation from service that are made after age 55.
- The exception for qualified domestic relations orders (QDROs) does not apply (although a special rule applies under which, as part of a divorce or separation agreement, a tax-free transfer may be made directly to an IRA of a spouse or former spouse).
- The exception for payments made at least annually in equal or close to equal amounts over a specified period applies without regard to whether you have had a separation from service.

- There are additional exceptions for (1) payments for qualified higher education expenses, (2) payments up to $10,000 used in a qualified first-time home purchase, and (3) payments after you have received unemployment compensation for 12 consecutive weeks (or would have been eligible to receive unemployment compensation but for self-employed status).

Will I owe State income taxes?

This notice does not describe any State or local income tax rules (including withholding rules).

SPECIAL RULES AND OPTIONS

If your payment includes after-tax contributions

After-tax contributions included in a payment are not taxed. If a payment is only part of your benefit, an allocable portion of your after-tax contributions is generally included in the payment. If you have pre-1987 after-tax contributions maintained in a separate account, a special rule may apply to determine whether the after-tax contributions are included in a payment.

You may roll over to an IRA a payment that includes after-tax contributions through either a direct rollover or a 60-day rollover. You must keep track of the aggregate amount of the after-tax contributions in all of your IRAs (in order to determine your taxable income for later payments from the IRAs). If you do a direct rollover of only a portion of the amount paid from the Plan and a portion is paid to you, each of the payments will include an allocable portion of the after-tax contributions. If you do a 60-day rollover to an IRA of only a portion of the payment made to you, the after-tax contributions are treated as rolled over last. For example, assume you are receiving a complete distribution of your benefit which totals $12,000, of which $2,000 is after-tax contributions. In this case, if you roll over $10,000 to an IRA in a 60-day rollover, no amount is taxable because the $2,000 amount not rolled over is treated as being after-tax contributions.

You may roll over to an employer plan all of a payment that includes after-tax contributions, but only through a direct rollover (and only if the receiving plan separately accounts for after-tax contributions and is not a governmental section 457(b) plan). You can do a 60-day rollover to an employer plan of part of a payment that includes after-tax contributions, but only up to the amount of the payment that would be taxable if not rolled over.

If you miss the 60-day rollover deadline

Generally, the 60-day rollover deadline cannot be extended. However, the IRS has the limited authority to waive the deadline under certain extraordinary circumstances, such as when external events prevented you from completing the rollover by the 60-day rollover deadline. To apply for a waiver, you must file a private letter ruling request with the IRS. Private letter ruling requests require the payment of a nonrefundable user fee. For more information, see IRS Publication 590, Individual Retirement Arrangements (IRAs).

If your payment includes employer stock that you do not roll over

If you do not do a rollover, you can apply a special rule to payments of employer stock (or other employer securities) that are either attributable to after-tax contributions or paid in a lump sum after separation from service (or after age 59½, disability, or the participant's death). Under the special rule, the net unrealized appreciation on the stock will not be taxed when distributed from the Plan and will be taxed at capital gain rates when you sell the stock. Net unrealized appreciation is generally the increase in the value of employer stock after it was acquired by the Plan. If you do a rollover for a payment that includes employer stock (for example, by selling the stock and rolling over the proceeds within 60 days of the payment), the special rule relating to the distributed employer stock will not apply to any subsequent payments from the IRA or employer plan. The Plan administrator can tell you the amount of any net unrealized appreciation.

If you have an outstanding loan that is being offset

If you have an outstanding loan from the Plan, your Plan benefit may be offset by the amount of the loan, typically when your employment ends. The loan offset amount is treated as a distribution to you at the time of the offset and will be taxed (including the 10% additional income tax on early distributions, unless an exception applies) unless you do a 60-day rollover in the amount of the loan offset to an IRA or employer plan.

If you were born on or before January 1, 1936

If you were born on or before January 1, 1936 and receive a lump sum distribution that you do not roll over, special rules for calculating the amount of the tax on the payment might apply to you. For more information, see IRS Publication 575, Pension and Annuity Income.

If your payment is from a governmental section 457(b) plan

If the Plan is a governmental section 457(b) plan, the same rules described elsewhere in this notice generally apply, allowing you to roll over the payment to an IRA or an employer plan that accepts rollovers. One difference is that, if you do not do a rollover, you will not have to pay the 10% additional income tax on early distributions from the Plan even if you are under age 59½ (unless the payment is from a separate account holding rollover contributions that were made to the Plan from a tax-qualified plan, a section 403(b) plan, or an IRA). However, if you do a rollover to an IRA or to an employer plan that is not a governmental section 457(b) plan, a later distribution made before age 59½ will be subject to the 10% additional income tax on early distributions (unless an exception applies). Other differences are that you cannot do a rollover if the payment is due to an "unforeseeable emergency" and the special rules under "If your payment includes employer stock that you do not roll over" and "If you were born on or before January 1, 1936" do not apply.

If you are an eligible retired public safety officer and your pension payment is used to pay for health coverage or qualified long-term care insurance

If the Plan is a governmental plan, you retired as a public safety officer, and your retirement was by reason of disability or was after normal retirement age, you can exclude from your taxable income plan payments paid directly as premiums to an accident or health plan (or a qualified long-term care insurance contract) that your employer maintains for you, your spouse, or your dependents, up to a maximum of $3,000 annually. For this purpose, a public safety officer is a law enforcement officer, firefighter, chaplain, or member of a rescue squad or ambulance crew.

If you roll over your payment to a Roth IRA

You can roll over a payment from the Plan made before January 1, 2010 to a Roth IRA only if your modified adjusted gross income is not more than $100,000 for the year the payment is made to you and, if married, you file a joint return. These limitations do not apply to payments made to you from the Plan after 2009. If you wish to roll over the payment to a Roth IRA, but you are not eligible to do a rollover to a Roth IRA until after 2009, you can do a rollover to a traditional IRA and then, after 2009, elect to convert the traditional IRA into a Roth IRA.

If you roll over the payment to a Roth IRA, a special rule applies under which the amount of the payment rolled over (reduced by any after-tax amounts) will be taxed. However, the 10% additional income tax on early distributions will not apply (unless you take the amount rolled over out of the Roth IRA within 5 years, counting from January 1 of the year of the rollover). For payments from the Plan during 2010 that are rolled over to a Roth IRA, the taxable amount can be spread over a 2-year period starting in 2011.

If you roll over the payment to a Roth IRA, later payments from the Roth IRA that are qualified distributions will not be taxed (including earnings after the rollover). A qualified distribution from a Roth IRA is a payment made after you are age 59½ (or after your death or disability, or as a qualified first-time homebuyer distribution of up to $10,000) and after you have had a Roth IRA for at least 5 years. In applying this 5-year rule, you count from January 1 of the year for which your first contribution was made to a Roth IRA. Payments from the Roth IRA that are not qualified distributions will be taxed to the extent of earnings after the rollover, including the 10% additional income tax on early distributions (unless an exception applies). You do not have to take required minimum distributions from a Roth IRA during your lifetime. For more information, see IRS Publication 590, Individual Retirement Arrangements (IRAs).

You cannot roll over a payment from the Plan to a designated Roth account in an employer plan.

If you are not a plan participant

Payments after death of the participant. If you receive a distribution after the participant's death that you do not roll over, the distribution will generally be taxed in the same manner described elsewhere in this notice. However, the 10% additional income tax on early distributions and the special rules for public safety officers do not apply, and the special rule described under the section "If you were born on or before January 1, 1936" applies only if the participant was born on or before January 1, 1936.

If you are a surviving spouse. If you receive a payment from the Plan as the surviving spouse of a deceased participant, you have the same rollover options that the participant would have had, as described elsewhere in this notice. In addition, if you choose to do a rollover to an IRA, you may treat the IRA as your own or as an inherited IRA.

An IRA you treat as your own is treated like any other IRA of yours, so that payments made to you before you are age 59½ will be subject to the 10% additional income tax on early distributions (unless an exception applies) and required minimum distributions from your IRA do not have to start until after you are age 70½.

If you treat the IRA as an inherited IRA, payments from the IRA will not be subject to the 10% additional income tax on early distributions. However, if the participant had started taking required minimum distributions, you will have to receive required minimum distributions from the inherited IRA. If the participant had not started taking required minimum distributions from the Plan, you will not have to start receiving required minimum distributions from the inherited IRA until the year the participant would have been age 70½.

If you are a surviving beneficiary other than a spouse. If you receive a payment from the Plan because of the participant's death and you are a designated beneficiary other than a surviving spouse, the only rollover option you have is to do a direct rollover to an inherited IRA. Payments from the inherited IRA will not be subject to the 10% additional income tax on early distributions. You will have to receive required minimum distributions from the inherited IRA.

Payments under a qualified domestic relations order. If you are the spouse or former spouse of the participant who receives a payment from the Plan under a qualified domestic relations order (QDRO), you generally have the same options the participant would have (for example, you may roll over the payment to your own IRA or an eligible employer plan that will accept it). Payments under the QDRO will not be subject to the 10% additional income tax on early distributions.

If you are a nonresident alien

If you are a nonresident alien and you do not do a direct rollover to a U.S. IRA or U.S. employer plan, instead of withholding 20%, the Plan is generally required to withhold 30% of the payment for federal income taxes. If the amount withheld exceeds the amount of tax you owe (as may happen if you do a 60-day rollover), you may request an income tax refund by filing Form 1040NR and attaching your Form 1042-S. See Form W-8BEN for claiming that you are entitled to a reduced rate of withholding under an income tax treaty. For more information, see also IRS Publication 519, U.S. Tax Guide for Aliens, and IRS Publication 515, Withholding of Tax on Nonresident Aliens and Foreign Entities.

Other special rules

If a payment is one in a series of payments for less than 10 years, your choice whether to make a direct rollover will apply to all later payments in the series (unless you make a different choice for later payments).

If your payments for the year are less than $200 (not including payments from a designated Roth account in the Plan), the Plan is not required to allow you to do a direct rollover and is not required to withhold for federal income taxes. However, you may do a 60-day rollover.

Unless you elect otherwise, a mandatory cashout of more than $1,000 (not including payments from a designated Roth account in the Plan) will be directly rolled over to an IRA chosen by the Plan administrator or the payor. A mandatory cashout is a payment from a plan to a participant made before age 62 (or normal retirement age, if later) and without consent, where the participant's benefit does not exceed $5,000 (not including any amounts held under the plan as a result of a prior rollover made to the plan).

You may have special rollover rights if you recently served in the U.S. Armed Forces. For more information, see IRS Publication 3, Armed Forces' Tax Guide.

FOR MORE INFORMATION

You may wish to consult with the Plan administrator or payor, or a professional tax advisor, before taking a payment from the Plan. Also, you can find more detailed information on the federal tax treatment of payments from employer plans in: IRS Publication 575, Pension and Annuity Income; IRS Publication 590, Individual Retirement Arrangements (IRAs); and IRS Publication 571, Tax-Sheltered Annuity Plans (403(b) Plans). These publications are available from a local IRS office, on the web at www.irs.gov, or by calling 1-800-TAX-FORM.

* * *

End Notes

[1] For the purpose of this report, "rollover" generally refers to a distribution from a 401(k) plan that an individual moves into another employer-sponsored retirement plan or IRA, in order to avoid the funds being considered income and, thereby, immediately subject to income tax. Amounts taken from IRAs are generally referred to as "withdrawals," but to minimize confusion, in this report we use the term "distribution" with respect to IRAs as well as 401(k) plans.

[2] In this case, employer-sponsored retirement plans included defined contribution and defined benefit plans. Investment Company Institute, The U.S. Retirement Market, Second Quarter 2012 (September 2012). http://www.ici.org/info/ret_12_q2_data.xls.

[3] In this report we refer to a rollover from a 401(k) plan to another employer-sponsored retirement plan as a "plan-to-plan rollover."

[4] Employer contributions to qualified plans are a tax-deductible business expense, and, in general, contributions and investment earnings on those contributions are not taxed as income until the employee withdraws them from the plan.

[5] Pub. L. No. 93-406, 88 Stat. 829 (codified as amended at 29 U.S.C. §§ 1001-1461).

[6] 29 U.S.C. § 1002(2).

[7] 29 U.S.C. § 1003(35).

[8] 29 U.S.C. § 1002(34).

[9] See U.S. Department of Labor Employee Benefits Security Administration, Private Pension Plan Bulletin: Abstract of 2010 Form 5500 Annual Reports, Version 1.0 (Washington, D.C.: November 2012).

[10] Ibid.

[11] Employee Benefit Research Institute, *401(k) Plan Asset Allocation, Account Balances, and Loan Activity in 2009* (Washington, D.C.: November 2010).

[12] GAO, *Private Pensions: Changes Needed to Provide 401(k) Plan Participants and the Department of Labor Better Information on Fees*, GAO-07-21 (Washington, D.C.: Nov. 16, 2006).

[13] For more information on 401(k) plan service provider arrangements and fees see GAO, *401(k) Plans: Increased Educational Outreach and Broader Oversight May Help Reduce Plan Fees*, GAO-12-325 (Washington, D.C.: Apr. 24, 2012).

[14] U.S. retirement market assets are composed of assets in IRAs, defined contribution plans, private-sector defined benefit plans, state and local government pension plans, federal pension plans, and annuity reserves. In 2012, total U.S. retirement market assets were over $18 trillion, according to estimates from the Investment Company Institute, The U.S. Retirement Market, Second Quarter 2012 (September 2012), http://www.ici.org/info/ret_12_q2_data.xls.

[15] Pub. L. No. 105-34, § 302(a), 111 Stat. 788, 825-28 (codified as amended at 26 U.S.C. § 408A). There are also two types of employer-sponsored IRAs—Simplified Employee Pension (SEP) and Savings Incentive Match Plans for Employees (SIMPLE) (referred to in the IRC as a simple retirement account). 26 U.S.C. § 408(k) and (p), respectively. Under SEP IRAs, employers of any size make voluntary tax deductible contributions to traditional IRAs for themselves and their employees. Under SIMPLE IRAs, small employers match part of participating employees', generally tax-deductible, contributions, or make contributions for all eligible employees based on a fixed percentage of pay, to traditional IRAs. Contributions to all IRAs may not exceed certain limits. For more information on these types of plans, see GAO, *Individual Retirement Accounts: Government Actions Could*

Encourage More Employers to Offer IRAs to Employees, GAO-08-590 (Washington, D.C.: June 4, 2008). Employers can also offer both traditional and Roth IRAs established as payroll-deduction IRAs (also called payroll-deduction IRA programs). Through payroll-deduction IRAs, employees may establish and contribute to traditional or Roth IRAs through voluntary deductions from their pay, which are forwarded by the employer to the employee's IRA. As long as employers follow guidelines set by Labor for managing the payroll-deductions, such arrangements are not considered pension plans and employers are not, therefore, subject to the fiduciary standards under ERISA. Each of these IRAs has its own eligibility requirements. 29 C.F.R. § 2509.99-1 (also known as Interpretive Bulletin 99-1). In addition, employers may offer "deemed IRAs" to their employees, which allow employees to keep IRA assets in their employer's tax-qualified retirement plan as separate, traditional or Roth, IRAs. 26 U.S.C. § 408(q). Employees make voluntary contributions to the deemed IRA, subject to IRA rules. According to Treasury, few deemed IRAs exist.

[16] We use the term "cash out" to refer to a lump-sum distribution made to an employee at job separation that is not subsequently rolled over into a qualified employer plan or IRA. For more information on the effects of cash outs see GAO, *401(k) Plans: Policy Changes Could Reduce the Long-term Effects of Leakage on Workers' Retirement Savings*, GAO-09-715 (Washington, D.C.: Aug. 28, 2009).

[17] Not all plans accept rollovers from other plans. For detailed information on rollover eligibility for different plans, see http://www.irs.gov/pub/irs-tege/rollover chart.pdf. In some circumstances plan participants may choose a combination of options, such as leaving a portion of assets in the plan and taking a partial distribution. However, some participants have more limited options, and some plans automatically distribute plan balances under $5,000 to separating participants, although plans are prohibited from immediately distributing such balances without consent. 26 U.S.C. § 411(a)(11)(A). If a participant elects to have a mandatory distribution rolled over to a specific IRA, however, plans are required to make a direct rollover to that IRA. For mandatory distributions between $1,000 and $5,000, even if participants make no such elections, plans must automatically roll such distributions into an IRA on their behalf. 26 U.S.C. § 401(a)(31). Labor has a safe harbor regulation to guide plan fiduciaries in making such automatic rollovers. 29 C.F.R. § 2550.404a-2 (2012). Any money rolled over to a Roth IRA that was not previously in a designated Roth account in a plan will count towards an individual's gross annual income. Notice 2009-75, 2009-39 I.R.B. 436.

[18] 26 U.S.C. § 72(t). The IRC exempts certain early distributions, such as those made to a participant after separation from service with an employer after reaching age 55. 26 U.S.C. § 72(t)(2)(A)(v). For more information on exemptions from early distributions see http://www.irs.gov/Retirement-Plans/Plan-Participant,-Employee/Retirement-Topics---Tax-on-Early-Distributions and http://www.irs.gov/file_source/pub/irs-tege/early_distributions.pdf.

[19] As regular income distributions, these early distributions are also subject to federal income tax withholding and taxed at the marginal income tax rate.

[20] 26 U.S.C. § 3405(c)(1)(B).

[21] A direct rollover is when a participant specifies the plan or IRA to which their distribution should be transferred. The plan can transfer the money via non-transferable check made out to the receiving entity or electronically. The ability to transfer money electronically depends on the ability and policy of the distributing and receiving entities. Indirect rollovers are rollovers that are not direct rollovers.

[22] 26 U.S.C. § 402(c)(3).

[23] Stephen P. Utkus and Jean A. Young, *Distribution Decisions Among Retirement-age Defined Contribution Plan Participants,* The Vanguard Group, Inc. (December 2010).

[24] Investment Company Institute, The U.S. Retirement Market, Second Quarter 2012 (September 2012), http://www.ici.org/info/ret_12_q2_data.xls.

[25] In 2012, the median value of traditional IRAs with rollover funds was $62,500, compared with $30,000 for those without rollovers funds. Sarah Holden and Daniel Schrass, The Role of IRAs in U.S. Households' Saving for Retirement, 2012, *ICI Research Perspective* 18, no. 8 (December 2012). Available at www.ici.org/pdf/ per18-08.pdf.

[26] 29 U.S.C. §§ 1001b(a) and 1003(a), respectively.

[27] Under ERISA, persons are generally fiduciaries with respect to 401(k) plans, to the extent they exercise any discretionary authority or control over plan management or any authority or control over the management or disposition of plan assets, render investment advice respecting plan money or property for a fee or other compensation (or have the authority or responsibility to do so), or have discretionary authority or responsibility for plan administration. 29 U.S.C. § 1002(21)(A).

[28] 29 U.S.C. § 1104(a).

[29] In June 1996, EBSA issued an interpretive bulletin defining participant investment education, 61 Fed. Reg. 29,586, 29,589-90 (June 11, 1996) (codified at 29 C.F.R. § 2509.96-1(c) and (d)(2012)). The bulletin identified specific categories of investment-related information that, when furnished to plan participants or beneficiaries, would not constitute the rendering of investment advice under ERISA. The categories of information include the following: plan information; general financial and investment information; asset allocation models; and interactive investment materials.

[30] Advisory Op. 2005-23A (Dec. 7, 2005).

[31] 29 C.F.R. § 2509.96-1(d)(3) (2012).

[32] 75 Fed. Reg. 65,263.

[33] 76 Fed. Reg. 2,142, 2,143. Labor officials said the department received many comments, both pro and con, on whether the provision of investment advice should include recommendations to take a distribution and the effect of coupling such a recommendation with advice as to investing any distribution.

[34] 26 U.S.C. §§ 401-415. Such requirements include, for example, participation, vesting, and funding standards.

[35] 26 U.S.C. § 4975.

[36] 29 U.S.C. § 1006.

[37] 5 U.S.C. App. Statutory exemptions generally include, for example, certain loans to participants or beneficiaries, the provision of services needed to operate a plan for reasonable compensation, loans to employee stock ownership plans, and investment with certain financial institutions regulated by other state or federal agencies. 26 U.S.C. § 4975(d) and 29 U.S.C. § 1108(b).

[38] 26 U.S.C. § 408(e)(2). As a result, any funds not previously taxed will be subject to income tax but not to the tax otherwise imposed in the case of prohibited transactions. 26 U.S.C. § 4975(c)(3).

[39] State securities authorities have primary regulatory authority over investment advisers with less than $100 million of assets under management. For a more detailed discussion of securities regulation see GAO, *Financial Regulation: Industry Changes Prompt Need to Reconsider U.S. Regulatory Structure*, GAO-05-61 (Washington, D.C.: Oct 6, 2004) and GAO, *Consumer Finance: Regulatory Coverage Generally Exists for Financial Planners, but Consumer Protection Issues Remain,* GAO-11-235 (Washington, D.C.: Jan 18, 2011).

[40] Investment Advisers Act of 1940, 15 U.S.C. §§ 80b-1 – 80b-21. The Advisers Act defines an investment adviser as any person (i.e., individual or firm) who is in the business of providing advice, or issuing reports or analyses, regarding securities, for compensation. 15 U.S.C. § 80b-2(a)(11); IA Rel. No. 1092.

[41] 15 U.S.C. §§ 78a – 78pp. Broker-dealers are regulated by FINRA and by SEC under the federal securities laws and FINRA rules.

[42] The major securities industry self-regulatory organizations, such as FINRA, impose suitability rules that members must follow. For example, under former National Association of Securities Dealers Conduct Rule 2310, a FINRA member making an investment recommendation to a customer must have grounds for believing that the recommendation is suitable for that customer's financial situation and needs. In August 2010, FINRA proposed new consolidated rules governing the suitability obligations and know-yourcustomer obligations of its members. The new rules retain the core features of the current rules, while modifying both rules to strengthen and clarify them. On November 17, 2010, SEC approved the rule changes with slight modifications. Exchange Act Release No. 63325, 75 Fed. Reg. 71479 (Nov. 23, 2010). The new rule was effective on July 9, 2012.

[43] Pub. L. No. 111-203, § 913(b), 124 Stat. 1376, 1824-25 (2010) a retail customer is defined as a natural person, or the legal representative of a natural person, who receives personalized investment advice from a broker, dealer, or investment adviser and uses the advice primarily for personal, family, or household purposes.

[44] SEC, *Study on Investment Advisers and Broker*-Dealers (Washington, D.C.: January, 2011). In response to SEC's request for comments to inform its study, FINRA noted that there is no broker-dealer equivalent to the up-front general disclosure of an investment adviser's business activities and relationships that may cause conflicts of interest with retail customers. Letter from Marc Menchel, Executive Vice President and General Counsel, FINRA, to Elizabeth M. Murphy, Secretary, SEC, August 25, 2010.

[45] GAO, *401(k) Plans: Improved Regulation Could Better Protect Participants from Conflicts of Interest*, GAO-11-119 (Washington, D.C.: Jan. 28, 2011).

[46] 26 C.F.R. § 1.401(a)(31)-1, Q/A-14 (2012).

[47] Recordkeeping services, including processing transactions such as rollovers, are among the many services offered by 401(k) plan service providers.

[48] 26 C.F.R. § 1.401(a)(31), Q/A-4 (2012).

[49] Cogent Research, Investor Assets in Motion ™ 2012: IRA and Retirement Marketplace Opportunities (December 2011).

[50] Spectrem Group, IRA Rollover Market 2011. Those data were not generalizable, according to GAO standards for statistical reliability, and statements made describing those data reflect only the experience of the 940 individuals who responded to Spectrem's survey.

[51] Cogent Research, Investor Assets in Motion ™ 2012: IRA and Retirement Marketplace Opportunities. (December 2011).

[52] See GAO-11-119.

[53] 29 C.F.R. § 2509.96-1(d)(3) (2012). Asset allocation models include information and materials that provide an investor with models of asset allocation portfolios of hypothetical individuals with different time horizons and risk profiles. Such models are based on generally accepted investment theories that take into account the historical returns of different asset classes (e.g., equities, bonds, or cash) over defined periods of time. (For more information see GAO-11-119.) An asset allocation model could be valuable for investors by identifying how they can reduce investment risk by further diversifying their investments, which means reallocating money across a range of stocks, bonds, or cash investments.

[54] 29 C.F.R. § 2509.96-1(d)(3)(iii) and (iv) (2012). By not making a recommendation, a provider presumably avoids crossing the line into investment advice, which would trigger ERISA fiduciary standards.

[55] 29 C.F.R. § 2510.3-21(c)(1)(i) (2012).

[56] See GAO-11-119. Also, as mentioned previously, numerous studies have found that many Americans lack basic financial literacy, including an understanding of fundamental investment concepts, such as the benefits of compounding interest, risk diversification, and inflation, that are necessary for making well-informed decisions and evaluating recommendations.

[57] LIMRA, http://www.limra.com/newscenter/newsarchive/archivedetails.aspx?prid=259.

[58] See GAO-11-119 and GAO-11-235.

[59] We previously reported that many 401(k) plan sponsors were unaware of or did not fully understand both the fees charged to their plans and their participants as well as the fee arrangements used by plan service providers. See GAO-12-325.

[60] Because the ERISA definition of fiduciary is functional in nature, a plan sponsor or service provider may have plan fiduciary status when performing some roles or functions but not others. Fiduciary status under ERISA does not depend on a person's formal title or how a person identifies themselves. Parker v. Bain, 68 F. 3d 1131, 1139 (9th Cir. 1995).

[61] GAO-11-119; GAO, *Financial Literacy: Enhancing the Effectiveness of the Federal Government's Role*, GAO-12-636T (Washington, D.C.: Apr. 26, 2012), and *Retirement Savings: Better Information and Sponsor Guidance Could Improve Oversight and Reduce Fees for Participants*, GAO-09-641 (Washington, D.C.: Sept. 4, 2009).

[62] For example, FINRA Investor Education Foundation, *Financial Capability in the United States* (December 2009).

[63] GAO, *Financial Literacy: Enhancing the Effectiveness of the Federal Government's Role*, GAO-12-636T (Washington, D.C.: Apr. 26, 2012).

[64] State Street Global Advisors, Biannual DC Investor Survey (July 2012).

[65] For Roth IRAs, distributions made after age 591/2 are not subject to income tax. For traditional IRAs funded with non-deductible contributions, the portion of distributions attributable to contributions is not taxed but the portion of distributions attributable to earnings is taxed.

[66] About 20 percent of 401(k) plans also offer access to a self-directed brokerage window. At the end of the 1st quarter in 2011, 36 percent of IRA assets were in brokerage accounts, which amounts to $1.7 trillion in retirement assets.

[67] 401(k) plans are required, for example, to disclose information about administrative feels or expenses that may be charged against a participant's individual account. 29 C.F.R. § 2550.404a-5(c)(3) (2012). In addition, investment-related information must be provided in a format designed to facilitate comparison. 29 C.F.R. § 2550.404a-5(d)(2) (2012).

[68] 75 Fed. Reg. 64,910, 69,937-46 (Oct. 20, 2010) (codified at 29 C.F.R. §§ 2550.404a-5 and 2550.404c-1 (2012)).

[69] We have reported that many 401(k) plan participants incorrectly believed their plans were free, but Labor's 2010 401(k) fee disclosure rules are intended to correct that misperception. See GAO-12-325 and GAO, *Private Pensions: Changes Needed to Provide 401(k) Plan Participants and the Department of Labor Better Information on Fees*, GAO-07-21 (Washington, D.C.: Nov. 16, 2006).

[70] Some industry website tools allow retail investors to compare mutual funds in a similar way, once they choose which funds to compare.

[71] Information obtained from our investigator's calls to 30 401(k) service providers, 27 of which also offer IRAs, provides illustrative examples of the type of information callers might

receive when inquiring about rolling funds into an IRA or a 401(k) plan, but they may not be representative of the general service provider population. See appendix I for further details regarding our methodology.

[72] In multiple websites we reviewed, disclosure of other fees was located in small type font in footnotes on the webpage. For example, one website stated in the main body of information on fees that it had no fee for selling funds, but a footnote stated that the $49.95 fee would be charged on redemption of funds held for 90 days or less if they were purchased through a proprietary service.

[73] Plans provide these rules to new participants in a summary plan description. 29 U.S.C. § 1022.

[74] Callan Associates, *2011 Defined Contribution Trends Survey*; and FRC, a Division of Strategic Insight, *The Rollover Decision: Successful Strategies for Retaining Retirement Assets*. Another survey of plan sponsors found that 26 percent of respondents preferred separated participants leave the plan and another 41 percent had no preference. Aon Hewitt, *Leakage of Participants' DC Assets: How Loans, Withdrawals, and Cashouts Are Eroding Retirement Income (2011)*.

[75] The IRC prohibits plan sponsors from distributing accounts valued at greater than $5,000 without the separated participants' consent. 26 U.S.C. § 411(a)(11)(A).

[76] IRS rules limit a plan's ability to treat separated participants differently by providing that consent to a distribution is not valid if, under the plan, "significant detriment" would have been imposed on a participant, had the participant not consented to the distribution. 26 C.F.R. § 1.411(a)-11(2) (2012).

[77] Plan sponsors may discourage separating participants from leaving money in the plan for several reasons. For example, they may wish to avoid bearing a fiduciary duty to someone who is no longer an employee. In addition, there may be extra costs to the plan of providing all the required disclosures to an additional participant, such as hiring a service provider to develop the materials as well as to print and mail them to participants. Also, in some cases, retaining separated participants and their savings causes the number of participants or amount of assets in the plan to exceed the threshold requiring a Form 5500 disclosure, a detailed disclosure that plans with 100 or more participants must submit annually to Labor. 29 U.S.C. § 1024(a)(1) and (2) and 29 C.F.R. § 2520.104-41 (2012). Meeting that requirement also adds to a plan's costs.

[78] Required Minimum Distributions are amounts that a retirement plan generally must distribute to an account owner annually starting with the year that he or she reaches 701/2 years of age or, if later, the year in which he or she retires. 26 U.S.C. § 401(a)(9)(A) and (C). If the retirement plan account is an IRA, the required minimum distribution must begin as soon as the account holder is 701/2 regardless of whether he or she is retired. 26 U.S.C. § 401(a)(9)(C)(i)(II).

[79] The IRC requires that participants with an eligible rollover distribution have the option to roll their distributions into an IRA or another employer's tax-qualified plan in the form of a direct rollover. 26 U.S.C. § 401(a)(31)(A).

[80] 26 U.S.C. § 72(t). The additional 10 percent tax will not apply to the early distributions from a 401(k) plan if any of various conditions are met. For example, if the distribution is made to a beneficiary (or to the estate of the participant) on or after the death of the participant. (For more information see www.irs.gov/retirement One of nine circumstances that exempts an IRA distribution from the 10 percent tax and that differs from the treatment of 401(k) plans, is if the distribution is a "qualified first-time homebuyer distribution." 26 U.S.C. § 72(t)(2)(F). (For more information see www.irs.gov/taxtopics/tc557.html.)

[81] 26 U.S.C. § 402(f)(1). The "402(f) special tax notice" explains the tax implications of the different distribution options, including explanation of the rollover rules, the special tax treatment for cash-outs (also called lump-sum distributions), and the mandatory withholding of 20 percent of distributions (including those that result in an indirect rollover). IRS regulations generally require plan sponsors to provide the "section 402(f) notice" to participants no less than 30 and no more than 90 days before the date of distribution. 26 C.F.R. § 1.402(f)-1, Q/A-2, Q/A-5) (2012). The Pension Protection Act of 2006 directed that these IRS regulations be modified to substitute 180 days for 90 days but no such regulation has been finalized. Pub. L. No. 109-280, § 1102(a)(1)(B), 120 Stat. 780, 1056.

[82] 26 C.F.R. §1.411(a)-11(c) (2012). IRS regulations generally require plan sponsors to also provide this information to participants no less than 30 and no more than 90 days before the date of distribution. The Pension Protection Act of 2006 directed that these IRS regulations be modified to substitute 180 days for 90 days but no such regulation has been finalized. Pub. L. No. 109-280, § 1102(a)(1)(B), 120 Stat. 780, 1056.

[83] 73 Fed. Reg. 59,575, 59,577 (Oct. 9, 2008). The proposed rule was also responding to requirements in the Pension Protection Act of 2006 that Treasury modify its regulations to provide that any description in a notice to participants of their right to defer receipt of a distribution also describe the consequences of failing to defer such receipt. Pub. L. No. 109-280, § 1102(b), 120 Stat. 780, 1056.

[84] Because of methodological limitations associated with the survey conducted with PLANSPONSOR and Society for Human Resource Management, results from the survey represent only the views of the 76 survey respondents. See appendix I for further details regarding our methodology.

[85] 29 U.S.C. § 1146. According to Labor, its *Saving Matters* education campaign uses a variety of formats to inform plan sponsors and participants on the importance of saving for retirement through workplace retirement plans and the agency also reaches out to plan sponsors to make them aware of ERISA and to help them understand their fiduciary responsibilities. The agency also reports that every year its Benefits Advisors help hundreds of thousands of plan participants who call Labor with questions about their retirement plan, including benefits distributions.

[86] We reviewed Labor's website, specifically the page on consumer information for retirement plans, on January 19, 2013. http://www.dol.gov/ebsa/consumer_info_pension.html.

End Notes for Appendix I

[1] We defined small plans as those with under 100 participants, medium plans as those with 100-4,999 participants, and large plans as those with 5,000 or more participants.

[2] View a video of our undercover phone calls to 401(k) plan service providers at http://www.gao.gov/multimedia

In: 401(k) Plans
Editor: Rudolph Graham

ISBN: 978-1-63482-669-3

Chapter 2

A LOOK AT 401(K) PLAN FEES*

Employee Benefits Security Administration

INTRODUCTION

More and more employees are investing in their futures through 401(k) plans. Employees who participate in 401(k) plans assume responsibility for their retirement income by contributing part of their salary and, in many instances, by directing their own investments.

If you are among those who direct your investments, you will need to consider the investment objectives, the risk and return characteristics, and the performance over time of each investment option offered by your plan in order to make sound investment decisions. Fees and expenses are one of the factors that will affect your investment returns and will impact your retirement income.

The information contained in this chapter answers some common questions about the fees and expenses that may be paid by your 401(k) plan. It highlights the most common fees and encourages you, as a 401(k) plan participant, to:

- Make informed investment decisions;
- Consider fees as one of several factors in your decision making;

---

* This is an edited, reformatted and augmented version of a document issued by the U.S. Department of Labor, August 2013.

- Compare all services received with the total cost; and
- Realize that cheaper is not necessarily better.

Keep in mind, however, that this chapter is a simplified explanation of some common 401(k) fees. It is not a legal interpretation of the nation's major retirement benefits protection law, the Employee Retirement Income Security Act (ERISA), or other laws, nor is this information intended to be investment advice.

1. Why Consider Fees?

In a 401(k) plan, your account balance will determine the amount of retirement income you will receive from the plan. While contributions to your account and the earnings on your investments will increase your retirement income, fees and expenses paid by your plan may substantially reduce the growth in your account which will reduce your retirement income. The following example demonstrates how fees and expenses can impact your account.

Assume that you are an employee with 35 years until retirement and a current 401(k) account balance of $25,000. If returns on investments in your account over the next 35 years average 7 percent and fees and expenses reduce your average returns by 0.5 percent, your account balance will grow to $227,000 at retirement, even if there are no further contributions to your account. If fees and expenses are 1.5 percent, however, your account balance will grow to only $163,000. The 1 percent difference in fees and expenses would reduce your account balance at retirement by 28 percent.

In recent years, there has been a dramatic increase in the number of investment options typically offered under 401(k) plans as well as the level and types of services provided to participants. These changes give today's employees who direct their 401(k) investments greater opportunity than ever before to affect their retirement savings. As a participant you may welcome the variety of investment options and the additional services, but you may not be aware of their cost. As shown above, the cumulative effect of the fees and expenses on your retirement savings can be substantial.

You should be aware that your employer also has a specific obligation to consider the fees and expenses paid by your plan. ERISA requires employers to follow certain rules in managing 401(k) plans. Employers are held to a high standard of care and diligence and must discharge their duties solely in the interest of the plan participants and their beneficiaries. Among other things, this means that employers must:

- Establish a prudent process for selecting investment options and service providers;
- Ensure that fees paid to service providers and other expenses of the plan are reasonable in light of the level and quality of services provided;
- Select investment options that are prudent and adequately diversified;
- Disclose plan, investment and fee information to participants to make informed decisions regarding their investment options under the plan; and
- Monitor investment options and service providers once selected to make sure that they continue to be appropriate choices.

2. What Are 401(K) Plan Fees and Who Pays for Them?

If you want to know how fees affect your retirement savings, you will need to know about the different types of fees and expenses and the different ways in which they are charged.

401(K) Plan Fees and Expenses Generally Fall into Three Categories

Plan administration fees. The day-to-day operation of a 401(k) plan involves expenses for basic administrative services – such as plan recordkeeping, accounting, legal and trustee services – that are necessary for administering the plan as a whole. Today, a 401(k) plan also may offer a host of additional services, such as telephone voice-response systems, access to a customer service representative, educational seminars, retirement planning software, investment advice, electronic access to plan information, daily valuation and online transactions.

In some instances, the costs of administrative services will be covered by investment fees that are deducted directly from investment returns. Otherwise, if administrative costs are separately charged, they will be borne either by your employer or charged directly against the assets of the plan. When paid directly by the plan, administrative fees are either allocated among participant's individual accounts in proportion to each account balance (i.e., participants with larger account balances pay more of the allocated expenses) or passed through as a flat fee against each participant's account. Either way, generally the more services provided, the higher the fees.

Investment fees. By far the largest component of 401(k) plan fees and expenses is associated with managing plan investments. Fees for investment management and other investment-related services generally are assessed as a percentage of assets invested. You should pay attention to these fees. You pay for them in the form of an indirect charge against your account because they are deducted directly from your investment returns. Your net total return is your return after these fees have been deducted.

Individual service fees. In addition to overall administrative expenses, there may be individual service fees associated with optional features offered under a 401(k) plan. Individual service fees are charged separately to the accounts of participants who choose to take advantage of a particular plan feature. For example, individual service fees may be charged to a participant for taking a loan from the plan or for executing participant investment directions.

401(K) Plan Investments and Services May Be Provided Through a Variety of Arrangements

Employers may directly provide, or separately negotiate with and hire different providers for, some or all of the various services and investment alternatives offered under their 401(k) plans (sometimes referred to as an unbundled arrangement). The expenses of each provider (i.e., investment manager, trustee, recordkeeper, communications firm) are charged separately.

In many plans, some or all of the various services and investment options may be offered by one provider for a fee paid to that provider (sometimes referred to as a bundled arrangement). The provider will then pay out of that fee any other service providers that it contracts with to provide the services.

Some plans may use an arrangement that combines a single provider for certain services, such as administrative services, with a number of providers for investment options. Regardless of the arrangement used, fees need to be evaluated, keeping in mind the cost of all covered services.

3. What Fees Are Associated with My Investment Choices in a 401(K) Plan?

Apart from fees charged for administration of the plan itself, there are three basic types of fees that may be charged in connection with investment options in a 401(k) plan. These fees, which can be referred to by different terms, include:

- Sales charges (also known as *loads or commissions)*. These are transaction costs for buying and selling of shares. They may be computed in different ways, depending upon the particular investment product.
- *Management fees* (also known as *investment advisory fees or account maintenance fees*). These are ongoing charges for managing the assets of the investment fund. They are generally stated as a percentage of the amount of assets invested in the fund. Sometimes management fees may be used to cover administrative expenses. You should know that the level of management fees can vary widely, depending on the investment manager and the nature of the investment product. Investment products that require significant management, research and monitoring services generally will have higher fees.
- *Other fees.* This category covers services, such as recordkeeping, furnishing statements, toll-free telephone numbers and investment advice, involved in the day-to-day management of investment products. They may be stated either as a flat fee or as a percentage of the amount of assets invested in the fund.

In addition, there are some fees that are unique to specific types of investments. Following are brief descriptions of some of the more common investments offered under 401(k) plans and explanations of some of the different terminology and unique fees associated with them.

SOME COMMON INVESTMENTS AND RELATED FEES

Most investments offered under 401(k) plans today pool the money of a large number of individual investors. Pooling money makes it possible for individual participants to diversify investments, to benefit from economies of scale and to lower their transaction costs. These funds may invest in stocks, bonds, real estate and other investments. Larger plans, by virtue of their size, are more likely to pool investments on their own – for example, by using a separate account held with a financial institution. Smaller plans generally invest in commingled pooled investment vehicles offered by financial institutions. Generally, investment-related fees, usually charged as a percentage of assets invested, are paid by the participant.

Mutual funds. Mutual funds pool and invest the money of many people. Each investor owns shares in the mutual fund that represent a part of the mutual fund's holdings. The portfolio of securities held by a mutual fund is managed by a professional investment adviser following a specific investment policy. In addition to investment management and administration fees, you may find these fees:

- Some mutual funds assess sales charges (see above for a discussion of sales charges). These charges may be paid when you invest in a fund (known as a **front-end load**) or when you sell shares (known as a back-end load, deferred sales charge or redemption fee). A front-end load is deducted up front and, therefore, reduces the amount of your initial investment. A back-end load is determined by how long you keep your investment. There are various types of back-end loads, including some which decrease and eventually disappear over time. A back-end load is paid when the shares are sold (i.e., if you decide to sell a fund share when a back-end load is in effect, you will be charged the load).
- Mutual funds also may charge what are known as Rule 12b-1 fees, which are ongoing fees paid out of fund assets. Rule 12b-1 fees may be used to pay for commissions to brokers and other salespersons, to pay for advertising and other costs of promoting the fund to investors and to pay various service providers of a 401(k) plan pursuant to a bundled services arrangement. Some mutual funds may be advertised as "no-load" funds. This can mean that there is no front- or back-end load. However, there may be a 12b-1 fee.
- Target date retirement funds, which are often mutual funds, hold stocks, bonds, and cash investments. These funds are designed to make investing for retirement more convenient by automatically changing your investment mix or asset allocation over time. Target date funds may charge different fees even with the same target date. If a target date fund invests in other mutual funds (often called a "fund-of-funds"), fees may be charged by both the target date fund and the other funds.

Collective investment funds. A collective investment fund is a trust fund managed by a bank or trust company that pools investments of 401(k) plans and other similar investors. Each investor has a proportionate interest in the trust fund assets. For example, if a collective investment fund holds $10 million in assets and your investment in the fund is $10,000, you have a 0.1 percent interest in the fund. Like mutual funds, collective investment funds may have different investment objectives. There are investment management and administrative fees associated with a collective investment fund.

Variable annuities. Insurance companies frequently offer a range of investment options for 401(k) plans through a group variable annuity contract between an insurance company and an employer on behalf of a plan. The variable annuity contract "wraps" around investment options, often a number of mutual funds. Participants select from among the investment options offered, and the returns to their individual accounts vary with their choice of investments. Variable annuities also include one or more insurance elements, which are not present in other investment options. Generally, these elements include an annuity feature, interest and expense guarantees, and any death benefit provided during the term of the contract. In addition to investment management fees and administration fees, you may find these fees:

- Insurance-related charges are associated with investment options that include an insurance component. They include items such as sales expenses, mortality risk charges and the cost of issuing and administering contracts.
- Surrender and transfer charges are fees an insurance company may charge when an employer terminates a contract (in other words, withdraws the plan's investment) before the term of the contract expires or if you withdraw an amount from the contract. This fee may be imposed if these events occur before the expiration of a stated period, and commonly decrease and disappear over time. It is similar to an early withdrawal penalty on a bank certificate of deposit or to a back-end load or redemption fee charged by some mutual funds.

Stable value funds. A common investment option that generally includes fixed income securities and one or more contracts issued by banks or insurance companies that provide protection of contributions invested (the principal) and accumulated interest, as well as a rate of return that may be fixed, linked to an index, or reset periodically based on the performance of the fund's investments. These funds may have investment management and other administrative fees associated with their operation.

While the investments described above are common, 401(k) plans also may offer other investments which are not described here (such as employer securities).

4. Where Can I Get Information About the Fees and Expenses Charged to My 401(K) Plan Account?

If you have questions about the fees and expenses charged to your 401(k) plan, review the documents noted below or contact your plan administrator.

The following information is available from your plan:

- If you direct the investments in your account, your plan will provide information about your rights and responsibilities under the plan related to directing your investments. This includes plan and investment-related information, including information about fees and expenses, that you need to make informed decisions about the management of your account. The investment-related information is provided in a format, such as a chart, that allows for comparison among the plan's investment options. The plan should provide this information before you can direct investments for the first time and annually thereafter. You also will receive a statement with information on fees and expenses for administrative or individual services actually paid from your individual account at least quarterly. This statement does not include charges paid indirectly from the investment options you have chosen.

  A model chart that is similar to what you may receive is included in the back of this publication. It includes performance data for each investment option over 1, 5 and 10 years; returns of an appropriate broad-based securities market index (referred to as a benchmark) over these same time periods for comparison; and fee and expense information on the costs of running each investment option (expense ratio) and service and shareholder-type fees (such as sales charges). The chart also includes a glossary to help you understand the investment options offered by your plan.

  To help you use this information, see EBSA's publication *Maximize Your Retirement Savings – Tips on Using the Fee and Investment Information From Your Retirement Plan.* These tips also will help you use the periodic fee and investment information from your plan to see if you want to make any changes.

- Your 401(k) plan's *summary plan description (SPD)* will tell you what the plan provides and how it operates. It may tell you about the investments offered by your plan, the fees and expenses paid by the plan, and how those expenses are allocated among plan participants. A copy of the SPD is furnished to participants when they join a plan and then every 5 years if there are material modifications or every 10 years if there is no modification.
- The plan's *annual report (Form 5500 series)* contains information regarding the plan's assets, liabilities, income and expenses and shows the aggregate administrative fees and other expenses paid by the plan. However, it will not show expenses deducted from investment results or fees and expenses paid by your individual account. You may examine the annual report for free online at *www.efast.dol.gov*. In general, the *summary annual report*, which summarizes the annual report information, is distributed each year.

You also may request copies of prospectuses or similar documents from your plan as well as financial statements provided to your plan, and share values for your plan's investment options (with the valuation date). In addition, you may want to consult the business section of major daily newspapers, business and financial publications, rating services, the business librarian at the public library, or the Internet (see the list of helpful Websites at the end of the this chapter.). These sources will provide information and help you compare the performance and expenses of your investment options with other investments outside of your 401(k) plan.

If, after doing your own analysis, you have questions regarding the rates of returns or fees of your plan's investment options, ask your plan administrator for an explanation.

5. What Other Factors Might Impact the Fees and Expenses of My 401(K) Plan?

- Funds that are "actively managed" (i.e., funds with an investment adviser who continually researches, monitors, and actively trades the holdings of the fund to seek a higher return than the market) generally have higher fees. The higher fees are associated with the more active management provided and sales charges from the higher level of trading activity. While actively managed funds seek to provide higher returns than the market, neither active management nor higher fees necessarily guarantee higher returns.

- Funds that are "passively managed" generally have lower management fees. Passively managed funds seek to obtain the investment results of an established market index, such as the Standard and Poor's 500, by duplicating the holdings included in the index. Thus, passively managed funds require little research or trading activity.
- If the services and investment options under your plan are offered through a bundled program, then some or all of the costs of plan services may not be separately charged to the plan or to your employer. For example, these costs possibly may be subsidized by the asset-based fees charged on investments. Compare the services received in light of the total fees paid.
- Plans with more total assets may be able to lower fees by using special funds or classes of stock in funds, which generally are sold to larger group investors. "Retail" or "brand name" funds, which are also marketed to individual and small group investors, tend to be listed in the newspaper daily and typically charge higher fees. Let your employer know your preference.
- Optional features, such as participant loan programs and insurance benefits offered under variable annuity contracts, involve additional costs. Consider whether they have value to you. If not, let your employer know.
- Retirement plans, such as 401(k) plans, are group plans. Therefore, your employer may not be able to accommodate each employee's preferences for investment options or additional services.

6. Is There a Checklist I Can Use to Review My 401(K) Plan's Fees?

There is an array of investment options and services offered under today's 401(k) plans. Answers to the following 10 questions will help in gathering information about the fees and expenses paid by your plan. If you cannot find the answers, ask your plan administrator.

401(K) FEES CHECKLIST

1. What investment options are offered under your company's 401(k) plan?
2. Do you have all available documentation about the investment options under your plan and the fees charged to your plan?
3. What types of investment education are available under your plan?
4. What arrangement is used to provide services under your plan (i.e., are any or all of the services or investment options provided by a single provider)?
5. Do you and other participants use most or all of the optional services offered under your 401(k) plan, such as a participant loan program and insurance coverage?
6. If administrative services are paid separately from investment management fees, are they paid for by the plan, your employer, or are they shared?
7. Are the investment options tracking an established market index or is there a higher level of investment management services being provided?
8. Do any of the investment options under your plan include sales charges (such as loads or commissions)?
9. Do any of the investment options under your plan include any fees related to specific investments, such as 12b-1 fees, insurance charges, or surrender fees, and what do they cover?
10. Does your plan offer any special funds or special classes of stock (generally sold to larger group investors)?

This chapter is only the beginning of your educational process. You should ask questions and educate yourself about investments. Monitoring your current investment selections and reviewing the investment options offered under your plan are part of a process that you, as an informed participant, will need to undertake continually.

Keep in mind that the law requires the fees charged to a 401(k) plan be "reasonable" rather than setting a specific level of fees that are permissible. Therefore, the reasonableness of fees must be determined in each case.

IN CONCLUSION ...

When you consider the fees in your 401(k) plan and their impact on your retirement income, remember that *all services have costs.* If your employer has selected a bundled program of services and investments, *compare all services received with the total cost.*

Remember, too, that higher investment management fees do not necessarily mean better performance. Nor is cheaper necessarily better. *Compare the net returns relative to the risks among available investment options.*

And, finally, *don't consider fees in a vacuum.* They are only one part of the bigger picture including investment risks and returns and the extent and quality of services provided. Keep in mind the importance of diversifying your investments.

7. What Other Sources of Information Are Available?

Listed below are some organizations and their Websites, phone numbers and publications that can help in your research.

From the *Employee Benefits Security Administration:*

Maximize Your Retirement Savings – Tips on Using the Fee and Investment Information From Your Retirement Plan
Target Date Retirement Funds Investor Bulletin
What You Should Know About Your Retirement Plan
Savings Fitness: A Guide to Your Money and Your Financial Future Taking the Mystery Out of Retirement Planning

Website:
www.dol.gov/ebsa

Toll-free Publication Hotline:
1-866-444-3272

From the Securities and Exchange Commission:
Get the Facts on Saving and Investing
Invest Wisely - An Introduction to Mutual Funds
Ask Questions - Questions You Should Ask About Your Investments

Website:
www.sec.gov
Toll-free phone information service: 1-800-SEC(732)-0330

From the Board of Governors of the Federal Reserve System: Website:
www.federalreserve.gov

From the Comptroller of the Currency:
Website:
www.occ.gov
Toll-free Hotline:
1-800-613-6743

From the American Savings Education Council (ASEC):
Website:
www.choosetosave.org/asec
Phone:
(202) 659-0670

From the Certified Financial Planner Board of Standards:
Website:
www.cfp.net
Toll-free Hotline:
1-800-487-1497

From the Financial Industry Regulatory Authority:
Website:
www.finra.org
Phone:
(301) 590-6500

Model Comparative Chart

ABC Corporation 401k Retirement Plan

Investment Options – January 1, 20XX

This document includes important information to help you compare the investment options under your retirement plan. If you want additional information about your investment options, you can go to the specific Internet Web site address shown below or you can contact [insert name of plan administrator or designee] at [insert telephone number and address]. A free paper copy of the information available on the Web site[s] can be obtained by contacting [insert name of plan administrator or designee] at [insert telephone number].

DOCUMENT SUMMARY

This document has 3 parts. Part I consists of performance information for plan investment options. This part shows you how well the investments have performed in the past. Part II shows you the fees and expenses you will pay if you invest in an option. Part III contains information about the annuity options under your retirement plan.

Part I. Performance Information

Table 1 focuses on the performance of investment options that do not have a fixed or stated rate of return. Table 1 shows how these options have performed over time and allows you to compare them with an appropriate benchmark for the same time periods. Past performance does not guarantee how the investment option will perform in the future. Your investment in these options could lose money. Information about an option's principal risks is available on the Web site[s].

Table 1. Variable Return Investments

Name/ Type of Option	Average Annual Total Return as of 12/31/XX					Benchmark.		
	1yr	5yr	10yr.	Since Incep-tion	1yr.	5yr	10yr.	Since Inception
A Index Fund/ S&P 500 www. website address	26.5%	.34%	-1.03%	9.25%	26.46%	.42%	-.95% S&P 500	9.30%
B Fund/ Large Cap	27.6%	.99%	N/A	2.26%	27.80%	1.02%	N/A	2.77%

Name/ Type of Option	Average Annual Total Return as of 12/31/XX					Benchmark.		
	1yr	5yr	10yr.	Since Incep-tion	1yr.	5yr		
www. website address						US Prime Market 750 Index		
C Fund/ Int'l Stock	36.73%	5.26%	2.29%	9.37%	40.40 %	5.40%	2.40%	12.09%
www. website address						MSCI EAFE		
D Fund/ Mid Cap	40.22%	2.28%	6.13%	3.29%	46.29 %	2.40%	-.52%	4.16%
www. website address						Russell Midcap		
E Fund/ Bond Index	6.45%	4.43%	6.08%	7.08%	5.93%	4.97%	6.33%	7.01%
www. website address						Barclays Cap. Aggr. Bd.		
F Fund/ GICs	.72%	3.36%	3.11%	5.56%	1.8%	3.1%	3.3%	5.75%
www. website address					3-month US T-Bill Index			
G Fund/ Stable Value	4.36%	4.64%	5.07%	3.75%	1.8%	3.1%	3.3%	4.99%
www. website address					3-month US T-Bill Index			
Generations 2020/ Lifecycle Fund www. website address	27.94%	N/A	N/A	2.45%	26.46 %	N/A	N/A	3.09%
					S&P 500			
					23.95 %	N/A	N/A	3.74%
				Generations 2020 Composite Index*				

*Generations 2020 composite index is a combination of a total market index and a US aggregate bond index proportional to the equity/bond allocation in the Generations 2020 Fund.

Table 2 focuses on the performance of investment options that have a fixed or stated rate of return. Table 2 shows the annual rate of return of each such option, the term or length of time that you will earn this rate of return, and other information relevant to performance.

Table 2. Fixed Return Investments

Name! Type of Option	Return	Term	Other
H 200X/ GIC www. website address	496	2 Yr.	The rate of return does not change during the stated term.
I LIBOR Plus/ Fixed-Type Investment Account www. website address	LIBOR +296	Quarterly	The rate of return on 12/31/xx was 2.4596. This rate is fixed quarterly, but will never fall below a guaranteed minimum rate of 296. Current rate of return information is available on the option's Web site or at 1-800-yyy-zzzz.
J Financial Services Co./ Fixed Account Investment www. website address	3.7596	6 Mos.	The rate of return on 12/31/xx was 3.7596. This rate of return is fixed for six months. Current rate of return information is available on the option's Web site or at 1-800-yyy-zzzz.

Part II. Fee and Expense Information

Table 3 shows fee and expense information for the investment options listed in Table 1 and Table 2. Table 3 shows the Total Annual Operating Expenses of the options in Table 1. Total Annual Operating Expenses are expenses that reduce the rate of return of the investment option. Table 3 also shows Shareholder-type Fees. These fees are in addition to Total Annual Operating Expenses.

Table 3. Fees and Expenses

Name ! Type of Option	Total Annual Operating Expenses		Shareholder-Type Fees
	As a%	Per $1000	
Equity Funds			
A Index Fund/S&P 500	0.1896	$1.80	$20 annual service charge subtracted from investments held in this option if valued at less than $10,000.
B Fund/Large Cap	2.4596	$24.50	2.2596 deferred sales charge subtracted from amounts withdrawn within 12 months of purchase.
C Fund/International Stock	0.7996	$7.90	5.7596 sales charge subtracted from amounts invested.
D Fund/ Mid Cap ETF	0.2096	$2.00	4.2596 sales charge subtracted from amounts withdrawn.
Bond Funds			
E Fund/Bond Index	0.5096	$5.00	N/A
Other			
F Fund/GICs	0.4696	$4.60	1096 charge subtracted from amounts withdrawn within 18 months of initial investment.
G Fund/Stable Value	0.6596	$6.50	Amounts withdrawn may not be transferred to a competing option for 90 days after withdrawal.
Generations 2020/Lifecycle Fund	1.5096	$15.00	Excessive trading restricts additional purchases (other than contributions and loan repayments) for 85 days.
Fixed Return Investments			
H 200X / GIC	N/A		1296 charge subtracted from amounts withdrawn before maturity.
I LIBOR Plus/ Fixed-Type Invest Account	N/A		596 contingent deferred sales charge subtracted from amounts withdrawn; charge reduced by 196 on 12-month anniversary of each investment.
J Financial Serv Co. /Fixed Account Investment	N/A		90 days of interest subtracted from amounts withdrawn before maturity.

The cumulative effect of fees and expenses can substantially reduce the growth of your retirement savings. Visit the Department of Labor's Web site for an example showing the long-term effect of fees and expenses at http://www.dol.gov/ebsa/publications/401k_employee.html. Fees and expenses are only one of many factors to consider when you decide to invest in an option. You may also want to think about whether an investment in a particular option, along with your other investments, will help you achieve your financial goals.

Part III. Annuity Information

Table 4 focuses on the annuity options under the plan. Annuities are insurance contracts that allow you to receive a guaranteed stream of payments at regular intervals, usually beginning when you retire and lasting for your entire life. Annuities are issued by insurance companies. Guarantees of an insurance company are subject to its long-term financial strength and claims-paying ability.

Table 4. Annuity Options

Name	Objectives / Goals	Pricing Factors	Restrictions / Fees
Lifetime Income Option www. website address	To provide a guaranteed stream of income for your life, based on shares you acquire while you work. At age 65, you will receive monthly payments of $10 for each share you own, for your life. For example, if you own 30 shares at age 65, you will receive $300 per month over your life.	The cost of each share depends on your age and interest rates when you buy it. Ordinarily the closer you are to retirement, the more it will cost you to buy a share. The cost includes a guaranteed death benefit payable to a spouse or beneficiary if you die before payments begin. The death benefit is the total amount of your contributions, less any withdrawals.	Payment amounts are based on your life expectancy only and would be reduced if you choose a spousal joint and survivor benefit. You will pay a 2596 surrender charge for any amount you withdraw before annuity payments begin. If your income payments are less than $50 per month, the option's issuer may combine payments and pay you less frequently, or return to you the larger of your net contributions or the cash-out value of your income shares.

Table 4. (Continued)

Name	Objectives / Goals	Pricing Factors	Restrictions / Fees
Generations 2020 Variable Annuity Option www. website address	To provide a guaranteed stream of income for your life, or some other period of time, based on your account balance in the Generations 2020 Lifecycle Fund. This option is available through a variable annuity contract that your plan has with ABC Insurance Company.	You have the right to elect fixed annuity payments in the form of a life annuity, a joint and survivor annuity, or a life annuity with a term certain, but the payment amounts will vary based on the benefit you choose. The cost of this right is included in the Total Annual Operating Expenses of the Generations 2020 Lifecycle Fund, listed in Table 3 above. The cost also includes a guaranteed death benefit payable to a spouse or beneficiary if you die before payments begin. The death benefit is the greater of your account balance or contributions, less any withdrawals.	Maximum surrender charge of 896 of account balance. Maximum transfer fee of $30 for each transfer over 12 in a year. Annual service charge of $50 for account balances below $100,000.

Please visit www.ABCPlanglossary.com for a glossary of investment terms relevant to the investment options under this plan. This glossary is intended to help you better understand your options.

INDEX

E

F

G

H

I

S

T

U

V

W